€ 13.99
20/44
4

VOCAL STRENGTH & POWER

BOOST YOUR SINGING WITH PROPER TECHNI...

by Dena Murray

Back cover photo by BlackPixel.net

ISBN 978-1-4234-6514-0

HAL•LEONARD®
CORPORATION
7777 W. BLUEMOUND RD. P.O. BOX 13819 MILWAUKEE, WI 53213

In Australia Contact:
Hal Leonard Australia Pty. Ltd.
4 Lentara Court
Cheltenham, Victoria, 3192 Australia
Email: ausadmin@halleonard.com.au

Visit Hal Leonard Online at
www.halleonard.com

In her latest book, *Vocal Strength & Power*, Dena Murray brings her extensive experience as a vocal technique teacher and coach to the aid of singers working to improve or sustain their singing ability. The materials are suited for singers of all experience levels, from beginner to professional, and even instructors. Her writing style is direct, as is her approach to technique, introducing ideas in the same clear way she would explain them face to face.

In this newest offering, author Murray has extended her approach by discussing how the entire body works as a unit in singing.

Her first book, *Vocal Technique: A Guide to Finding Your Real Voice*, examines the character of the head and chest registers, with emphasis on strengthening the muscles that control the voice in both of those areas. This emphasis prepares for the connection of the registers into a seamless, continuous whole, and also introduces a way of training to induce proper engagement of the diaphragm without pushing.

The second book, *Advanced Vocal Technique: Middle Voice, Placement & Styles* (co-authored with Tita Hutchison), focuses on placement in the mask and how to bridge. By using perception of feeling and sensation, it builds a step-by-step progression from a thin to thicker voice without vocal "breaks."

In *Vocal Strength & Power*, Dena brings our attention to the diaphragm and especially to the *startling* results of her enquiry into how to teach proper vocal support without improper control and manipulation of that region. Together with her prior two books, this volume forms a complete set of exercises and understanding for bringing the voice to its full potential. When the elements are properly combined, the voice develops and problems are avoided. *Without* successful combination, the voice collapses, leading to eventual difficulties and uncomfortable singing.

Since singing technique is about doing some things and avoiding others, Dena's approach in this volume is very practical. In these pages, for each concept and singing action described, she provides exercises on the accompanying CD for self-paced practice to build habit.

The book is organized into sixteen content areas, beginning with her foundation concepts of the breath and engagement of the vocal cords. Once these core concepts are well-established, the middle chapters build and expand upon this foundation, connecting together thoughts on the speaking voice, resonance, projection, placement, self-diagnosis, muscle strength, and overall vocal coordination.

The latter chapters incorporate the more advanced topics of registers, consonant articulation, accomplishment of multiple vocal styles, and procedures that the student can use to master difficult words and song sections.

Rounding out this fine book are two sections of special interest: a comparison of breathing techniques for meditation vs. singing and a Glossary of voice-related terms.

D. Steven Fraser, Bachelors of Music Millikin University
Masters of Music (Choral Conducting), Washington University
Voice Council Charter Member, The Modern Vocalist

VOCAL STRENGTH & POWER
BOOST YOUR SINGING WITH PROPER TECHNIQUE & BREATHING
by Dena Murray

Introduction

Who Needs to Study Technique?

If you want more power in your voice, better pitch control, and a bigger singing range, then this book is for you. Even if you already have all these things, you can still benefit from this program, because every voice requires maintenance to prevent problems created by the heavy demands of professional singing.

Many famed singers sing instinctively, without thinking about it. Some of them will never take lessons because their voice is the one thing they know to have never failed them. Between their singing, performance skills, and their own brand of magic, they have become stars. A voice like this can hold up for perhaps a few years of professional singing, but without any training, there will soon come a time when the voice gives out. Many singers don't care and just change the keys of their previous works so they can still sing them. Others change their style somewhat so the voice is less taxed. Still others continue trying to sing the songs they once sang easily but aren't able to hit the high notes anymore. This either causes more damage or incites the audience to wish they'd just retire. All of these gifted performers and stylists who have never trained will at one time or another be faced with a choice: learn how to sing correctly, or lose the voice—sometimes the career.

About the CD

 **CD TRACK 1**

Warning: do **not** just pop the CD in your player and start singing along without reading the book! Each exercise has specific instructions of things to do and not do that you should understand before you even start. The CD tracks may extend beyond your range at either the high or low end (or both); everyone's vocal range is included. You should only sing the exercises in the keys you can handle while maintaining the correct prescribed technique to the best of your ability. Not doing so means you are working against yourself and eventually may cause more problems than you fix.

Pay attention to the CD track numbers listed before the exercises in the book. To minimize skipping around on your CD, all the practice tracks for men are grouped together, followed by those for women. Many of the exercises use different vowels and consonants with the same notes, so you will often be referred to the same piano track with a different assignment. The practice tracks are also structured to let you customize the exercises, letting you reuse the CD indefinitely. Short demo tracks come at the end of the CD so you can hear how each assignment should be performed.

The exercises are not meant for you to test or judge your abilities as a singer in any way. That happens in songs. The objective of the exercises is to retrain the reflexive actions of the various muscles of the vocal mechanism. We're reversing habits here, which takes time and repeated correction, just as if you were teaching yourself to stop cracking your knuckles or biting your nails.

How This Book Works

The word *knowledge* means understanding gained after one has learned from experience. In learning to sing correctly with good diaphragmatic support, yes, it's important to understand on an intellectual level what your internal vocal apparatus should be doing. But along with the explanations, you need to develop the reflexes needed for strong vocal technique with exercises that go step by step until you finally *know* how to do it. That's how this book is organized. Each step of the learning process is explained and drilled with an exercise. After the exercise, there is further discussion of things to consider at that stage of training.

Be prepared to stay on each exercise for weeks before moving on, and expect that you may sometimes need to go back to an exercise you've already practiced extensively. The study of voice is like that. Habits are hard to change, and they can creep back in at any time in your career.

Only think about the exercise *before* you actually practice it. During its performance, you should not be thinking hard; just pay attention to how it feels and how it sounds. Trying to figure it out, analyze it, and do it right all at once will not help you at all. Analyzing every little thing as you're trying to sing only makes the body tense up. If tensing becomes a sense-memorized habit, it'll prevent you from gaining the much-needed strength of the diaphragmatic muscle group regions. These are support structures for the sound-producing mechanism, the vocal cords. The only way to fully train for strengthening the support structures is to physically experience correct technique over and over again.

Nothing in this book should hurt your voice unless you have been unable to connect intellectually and physically with its instructions. If you are not actively taking lessons at this time, you are the one responsible for determining whether you understand the instructions in this book, or any other.

There are fine lines between excesses in either direction for many concepts in voice: edginess vs. breathiness, blowing breath vs. holding it. Often a student who is warned against doing too much of one thing will overcompensate by doing too much of another. We are striving for a balance that may even change between various styles of music.

Recording Your Practice

For technique practice, you need a cassette tape recorder that you can rewind easily. It doesn't have to be fancy, but don't get the tiny voice recorder that uses microcassettes. The speakers on those are not clear enough. I use a Radio Shack CTR-121 that uses regular cassettes and has a built-in microphone and a decent speaker. You're going to rewind and play back after each repetition or vocal run, listening for specific things depending on the exercise.

When listening to your tape, you will learn how to become the teacher. Let go of words like *good* and *bad*. Do not use words that undermine your confidence. These words do nothing to help. Instead, they keep you criticizing and judging yourself. If you thought you were a good singer before you began this new way of training but now judge and criticize every little sound, you'll walk away thinking you must have been crazy, can't sing, and were never able to.

Instead, evaluate your voice by using words like *correct* and *incorrect, right* or *wrong*. As you do so, it will help you move into the role of the teacher, with the voice your student. You might find with this change in word usage that you are now in competition with your voice and won't want to give up on it. You may even find yourself getting angry at the tape, as if it were a different person—especially when you listen back and hear mistakes. This is a good thing! It means you are challenging yourself to win. Eventually you will succeed. The voice will have to obey your commands because it will no longer be able to fight the will of your mind—no matter how hard your body fights to keep those bad (excuse me, I mean "incorrect") habits going.

Practice at least a half hour every day, five days a week. More is certainly okay. You can perform these exercises as long and as often as you like without fear of hurting yourself, because you're only trying to change incorrect habits. Just stop for the day if you find yourself getting frustrated. That way you'll still feel like practicing the next day.

I. Freeing the Diaphragm

3/4 VIEW DIAPHRAGM
APPROXIMATION

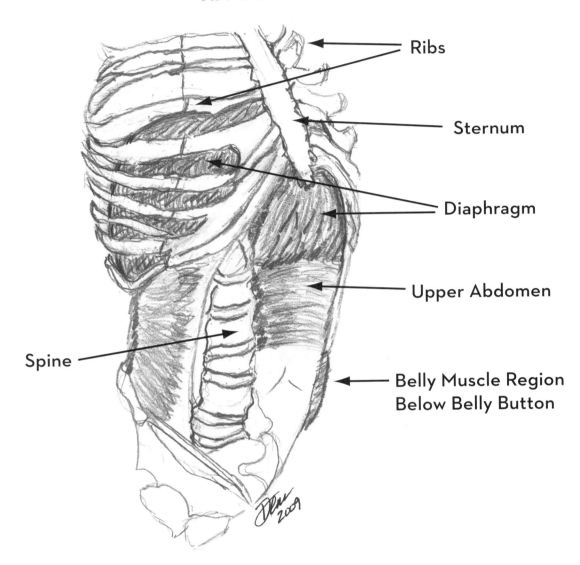

Ribs

Sternum

Diaphragm

Upper Abdomen

Spine

Belly Muscle Region
Below Belly Button

The diaphragm is a dome-shaped partition of muscles and tendons inside your ribcage that separates the chest from the abdominal cavity. It is below the lungs but above the stomach, intestines, and liver, so it is higher up in the torso than you might think.

The diaphragm needs to be able to position itself for the support needed to produce a strong and steady singing tone. This is brought about by proper inhalation. Unfortunately, instinct tells us to suck in as much air as possible and hold it before starting to sing. Such a survival-based instinct may be good for diving in the pool, but every singer must overcome it. Hard inhalation like this relies too much on other muscles attached to the pelvis, ribs, spine, shoulders, and neck, taking control away from the diaphragm and interfering with the vocal cords when singing.

The diaphragm moves downward on inhalation, pressing against the abdomen and its contents, causing it to bulge out. It is this bulging that leads many beginning singers to mistakenly believe that the abdominal muscles actually are the diaphragm. Upper abdominal expansion is only a consequence of having taken in air with the diaphragm. You shouldn't have to strain, tighten, or squeeze the lower belly region to manipulate this action. Similarly, when producing tone on the exhale, instinct may wrongly tell you to drive the air out with a blast by contracting those lower belly muscles to get the sound you want. This will actually produce weak sounds that easily go out of tune, and will eventually lead to damage of the vocal cords. The only way to gain the proper diaphragmatic support of the tone-producing mechanism is to train for it. All singers must learn how.

There are many vocal problems and many legitimate methods for fixing them in the world of vocal pedagogy. In my experience, however, most if not all of these problems have incorrect inhalation at their root, and the quickest and easiest way to fix them is to keep the student's attention focused on changing that habit above all else.

Take in a Little Bit of Air

Taking in heaps of air can be not only damaging, but it also brings on fatigue. See for yourself; draw in as much air as you can and then exhale it. Do this action over and over again for about five minutes. You're bound to feel a little tired—if you don't faint from hyperventilation! Now imagine breathing heavily and hard, in and out like this, but with sound, over and over again. Imagine having to do this between every couple of words or phrases for two sets on a gig. A tired singer's instinct will say, "You must inhale as much air as possible to keep that power, hit those high notes, and prolong the note for as much time as needed." Not so. It is unnecessary and will exhaust you. The vocal cords do not need much air to produce a strong tone.

 **CD TRACK 2**

EXERCISE 1. THE DOG PANT

This exercise helps break the habits of inhaling too much air at once, and closing the throat to hold onto the air once inhaled. In both the inhalation and exhalation parts of the exercise, the throat should stay relaxed and open. You don't need to think about the diaphragm, the abdomen, or your chest while you do this. Just concentrate on the quick in-out breath action. For this exercise and all others in the book, until otherwise instructed, remain in an upright seated position with both feet on the floor.

Ever watch a dog pant? They never use their entire body when panting. The breath goes straight into the mouth and comes right back out. It's a fairly quick action. They don't seem to need to take in very much in order to cool off. I imagine if a dog took the air all the way down into the belly, it would make it difficult to inhale and exhale at a fast pace. Instead of cooling off, they'd most likely overheat.

Let's start with lightly panting (breathing rapidly, hurriedly) in and out, through the mouth. Think of a dog that is about your size. Don't pant at the speed of a tiny Pekingese or you'll knock yourself out. Keep the breath short. The entire body does not need to get involved in order for you to take in enough air for the cords to do their job as the tone-producing mechanism. If you feel your shoulders rising, feel air stuck somewhere in your gut, tightness in the neck, or that that you have to shove the air out in order to keep breathing, then you've taken in too much.

Keep the Throat Open

In the dog pant exercise, the breath should feel as if it is circulating without interruption. If you feel yourself holding it between the inhale and exhale, even for a second, it's wrong. Holding the breath automatically closes the throat. Try it and see. Hold your breath for a second. As you are holding it, can you feel your neck tighten? Does it feel as though it would be easy to get air to pass by those cords without a push?

Hold your breath again and this time pay attention to your belly area. Does this area feel a bit constricted or tensed too? These things will occur when the throat automatically, like a reflex, slams shut to keep all the air from escaping too fast.

Upon attempting to get sound out from this completely closed condition, the cords will only be forced to open more than necessary to relieve the pressure. Too much breath pressure will make it difficult for the cords to hit their pitches and play their part in controlling the flow of air. The neck should never feel strained when singing. If you feel choked off at all, this indicates that you have taken the air in too deeply and/or too heavily. Reflex will have you trying to hold onto that air by grasping your neck and lower belly muscles to keep it from escaping.

The pressure (a sense impression created by the squeezing and constraining of too much air) will either force the pitch to become flat or sharp, or the sound to break and come out so distorted that you'll sound like a wannabe.

Exhale Immediately

Although we're not singing in the dog pant exercise, we're preparing for it. Sound must come out with air in an unwavering steady stream. When the air is inhaled and exhaled properly while singing, you should not feel any physical strain. In fact, the entire action of taking in a breath and singing all happens so fast that it will most likely take you by surprise. When experiencing it correctly, you will be astounded by how little air is needed to produce so many notes, or to enable you to sustain a note for a long time.

ACTION OF INHALE/EXHALE
APPROXIMATION
FEELS LIKE VS. ACTUAL

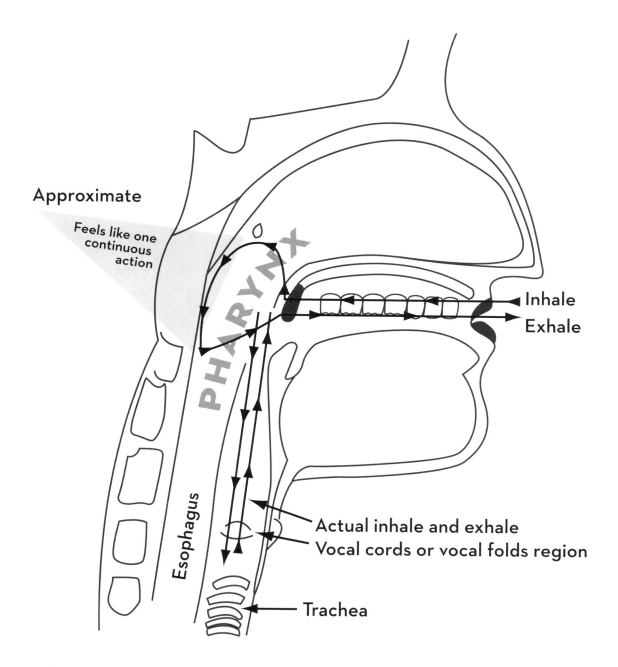

In the dog pant, the air should feel as if it's going straight to the back of your mouth and coming right back out again without any breaking action in between. This way of breathing trains the throat to stay open. If the intake has been performed correctly, the vocal cords will have received just enough air to control the flow and produce tones easily.

We'll inhale through the mouth when singing instead of through the nose for a few reasons. First, inhaling through the nose is slower and restricts the easy intake of air. Next, mouth inhalation helps keep the open-throat sensation that we want so that the neck muscles stay relaxed. Finally, when singing songs, we're going to focus our sounds at mouth level, though we will use the nasal pharynx to add resonance. For now, you just need to know that I want you to inhale through the mouth and not the nose when you practice these exercises, and keep that throat open!

Learning a New Way

Going from one way of breathing to another is difficult; it takes the ability to focus one's efforts on retraining. It requires repetitive practice of controlling exactly how much air is inhaled with the least amount of effort for maximum efficiency. The end result is correct support, which will give you freedom rather than discomfort, distorted sound, or pitch problems.

It's great if young singers start learning proper technique early on. However, if you are taking lessons because you think you should, the training and practice will not stick. Do you take lessons just because that's what singers are supposed to do? Why spend that kind of money and time if you already think you know how to sing, and everyone tells you so? Unfortunately, a gifted singer often only becomes teachable once something goes wrong. That's when they are hungry, open, willing, and can't get enough information.

Those who take lessons only out of a sense of duty have a tendency to think that if they've physically experienced something done correctly once, they will remember it; but when a body has sense-memorized a habit to do things one way, you can not expect it to change overnight. Practicing the "right way" to undo incorrect habits is the only way you will ever gain full control of your instrument and protect it from risk somewhere down the road.

II. Engaging the Vocal Cords

CD TRACK 3

EXERCISE 2. THE DESCENDING SIREN

This exercise teaches you to inhale exactly the right amount of air for the vocal cords to produce a long tone that moves from a high to a low pitch. It should sound a bit like the siren being turned off on a police car. You still don't need to be thinking about the diaphragm, abdomen, chest, or any other muscles yet.

Just before you begin, relax your body. It is with relaxation alone that you should release air. Try it. Hold your breath for a moment, then relax without blowing all of your air out at once. Did you notice that the air came out by itself? You only need to relax for leftover air to be released so that you can take in a new breath.

We will take in air in a similar way to the dog pant. When the inhalation is correct—just a small amount, without feeling like it's going all the way down into the belly—your vocal cords will immediately be able to come together, or *engage*, and work with the respiratory apparatus to control the flow of air while creating a long, steady, descending tone. If too much air is taken in before you start, you'll just blow it out when you start the sound, disengaging the cords and making the tone sound weak and un-musical at the beginning. Start wherever it is comfortable in your own range, from head voice going to the lowest note of your range. Finish the sound when you run out of all your air.

Start the Tone on the Tail End of the Inhaled Breath

Now take in a tiny short breath, keeping your throat open as in the dog pant. You'll immediately exhale a HUNNNNG sound with a descending tone.

Use the H to start the sound right behind the back of the tongue—not from the gut. This makes taking in the breath and exhaling with sound feel like it's occurring at almost the exact same moment. Another way of instructing this action is "start the tone on the tail end of the inhaled breath."

As soon as the tone starts, go right to the "NG" sound of the word. Don't spend much time on the "HU." Once the back of the tongue moves up to create the "NG" sound, it should stay where it is throughout the tone. The "NG" redirects the flow of air from the mouth to the nose. Because of this, you'll be less likely to try to blast the air out with force. Air will come out of the nose as you steadily descend all the way to the lowest of notes, but it may be nearly imperceptible.

It doesn't matter if the voice breaks while sirening. Right now the idea is to keep it going anyway, glitch or not. We'll address that area of weakness in the tone as we go along.

We are learning new habits that keep the very large diaphragmatic and abdominal muscles from overpowering the much smaller ones in the larynx. To that end, we'll assume that the job of controlling airflow goes to the vocal cords. In reality, the diaphragm and many other muscle groups (along with gravity, and multiple parts of the brain) do play a role in the control of breath pressure in a complex interaction.

No Straining, Please

Sometimes just knowing that sound is supposed to come out steadily may have you reflexively tightening your neck muscles to keep the air from escaping too fast. Some don't even realize that this is how they've been trying to gain control of their air. With time, it can become a habit that leads you to try to produce your high pitches by throat constriction instead of vocal cord function. This prevents the cords from developing their proper ability to come together for high notes—one of our ultimate goals in this book.

Just as with the dog pant, the inhale and exhale with this exercise must be contiguous— quickly switching from in to out with absolutely no break in between. This very quick combined action takes lots of practice. Continued careful repetitive practice will help you to unlearn the habit of taking in more air than necessary. The descending siren should help you sense-memorize this quick new action.

Keep Your Head Level

As you are vocalizing, keep your head level. Don't start dropping your chin down as the pitch lowers or you'll squish your larynx. Likewise, for the high-pitched beginning of the siren, don't raise your head. This will strain your neck muscles and constrict your throat. The head should always remain level when working on any exercise in this book.

Think First, Then Do

The learning process takes time, and old habits die hard. Sit with new ideas and contemplate them *before* you begin any vocalizing because they aren't things you'd normally pay attention to unless singing started feeling very uncomfortable. Even then, figuring out how to change discomfort to comfort may continue to be a mystery, especially on the higher notes. In not knowing how, most singers will just keep trying to grab those low belly muscles and take the air in even more heavily. All this does is produce results that are the same as before, if not worse, and reinforce incorrect habits.

III. Your Speaking Voice

What's Wrong in a Speaking Voice Can Show Up in Singing

Sometimes what is hindering the speaking voice from flowing naturally will also show up while singing. If you know you have a problem with pushing out your breath or holding the breath when you speak, then your singing voice might benefit from this next exercise. The next two CD tracks demonstrate exaggerated examples of these problems.

Blowing When Speaking

 **CD TRACK 4**

On this track, I took in a big breath, then forced it out as I spoke, which made me lose a lot of air in just those first three words or so. When speaking, just as in singing, only a relatively small amount of air is needed. When taking in a breath to begin a statement, you don't need to take in air so heavily that it goes all the way down into the bottom of your gut before you say something. Even though inhaling for speaking has always been an instinctive action, you may be taking in too much, which in turn leads you to lose it all by blowing it through your vocal cords as you begin to speak.

Holding the Breath and Squeezing When Speaking

 **CD TRACK 5**

Here, when I hold my breath and tighten my belly and neck muscles to speak, I feel like I don't have enough air and can't breathe by the time I've finished. When I squeeze like this, not only does my voice sound narrow and small, it also feels tight and strained.

For a variety of different possible reasons, many of us have learned to hold or squeeze the breath when speaking and aren't even aware of it until directed to pay attention to this tightness. If this is the case for you, you may also find the descending siren exercise difficult.

If you are unsure about whether you have either trouble when speaking, try feeling your body and listening as you speak. Does it feel tight? Does it sound squeezed, maybe choppy? If you notice that you run all of your sentences together and speak really fast, do you feel as though you are completely out of breath by the time you stop?

If air is forced, blown, or squeezed, you'll start running out of it quickly. You'll feel strain, and you'll sound choppy to those listening to you.

Relaxed Natural Speech

CD TRACK 6

Anytime you begin to speak, just as in singing, relax the front part of your torso just before you inhale. Again, it is in this split second of relaxation that any left over air is released before you take a breath for speaking. Air and sound should feel as if they start together, almost as one action.

Start the sound just behind the back of the tongue. If you're not used to starting your speech here, it can be a very strange sensation when you do. Some singers have been using so much body effort to sing that when they experience this "no body" feeling, they notice how little effort it takes. This makes them think, "This cannot possibly be right. It's too easy."

Ah, but learning exactly how to do this well on a consistent basis IS right. Learning to physically sense right from wrong while vocalizing or singing anything is the start of the road to vocal ease, and the freedom to express your artistic emotional self in songs.

Inhaling and exhaling, whether it is to speak or sing, should feel and sound as if it flows, and comes at a steady rate of speed—not in fits and spurts (unless you are using this style for effect).

EXERCISE 3. SPEAK WITHOUT HOLDING THE BREATH

Work on improving your speaking voice by reading aloud from a favorite book or magazine. Pay attention to punctuation. Besides its grammatical function, punctuation indicates when to pause, relax so that leftover air escapes, and then take in a new breath immediately before resuming. Always make sure you can feel yourself exhaling the words at a fairly steady rate of speed while reading aloud. Record yourself practicing the speaking voice fifteen minutes a day. Listen to the tape and determine if you took in too much air or held your breath at any time.

Doing this exercise will begin eliminating the habit of holding the breath. After a while, you should start to feel that speaking and singing are coming a bit easier, and with less anxiety spilling through. If the sound is fluidly moving, you may even find yourself feeling more calm and at peace.

If you've ever had problems getting people to listen to you, maybe you speak with a short, choppy quality that can be alienating those around you rather than bringing them closer in. When trying to get the attention of your friends or even get a word in edgewise in a conversation might be the time to test this theory. Calmly take in a tiny bit of air without squeezing anything, then begin talking. Listen for the flow of your words on exhale without blowing them out all at once. Take it easy. See if their response to you is any different, or if you have to resort to yelling one more time. Many have told me it works; people start listening.

IV. It's All About the Inhale

💿 **CD PRACTICE TRACK 7** • 54321 Men

💿 **CD TRACK 12** • 54321 Women

💿 **CD DEMO TRACK 17** • Staccato 54321 on HAH

EXERCISE 4. STACCATO 54321 ON HAH

Staccato sounds have distinct breaks through successive tones. In this exercise, the staccato may not be quite like staccato you've practiced in the past. Here, each note gets its own very quick little breath taken in just before, and connected to the sound.

Air is inhaled and exhaled similarly to the dog pant, but the pant is slightly slower in pace because it is performed with an actual major scale, descending through steps 5–4–3–2–1.

The very first time you try this exercise (also called a *vocalise*), you should listen to CD Demo Track 17, where I demonstrate along with the piano. As you work on the exercise in the future, just start right in on the practice track that's best for you: Track 7 or 12, and only go back to Track 17 if you need a reminder.

The exercise starts with the notes D–C–B–A–G, steps 5–4–3–2–1 of the G major scale. Then I move up a half step, to the key of A♭, and so on. The 25th run is too high for my voice, so I sit out through it, then come back in when I hear the same key where I left off before. You should do the same: only sing the exercise in the keys you can handle without pushing or straining.

After checking out the demo to hear what to do, men can then practice with Track 7, which moves through a range that may exceed some male voices, hitting a G above high C (G5 in scientific pitch notation) at its highest point on the 30th run. The track for female voices (Track 12) is the same as I used, starting in the key of G at D4 above middle C on the piano.

This exercise trains you to take in small amounts of air and then immediately exhale that air with a musical pitch. As long as you haven't taken in the air too heavily, you shouldn't have to think about it. The actions of both inhaling air and exhaling with sound should never come to a full stop or hesitation before reaching the end of a run. The throat must stay open throughout. Learning how to take in quick breaths like this is a much-needed skill for singing songs.

How It Happens

On inhalation, the belly (below the navel) will automatically become firm. Once firm, it should stay nearly unmoving until after you finish the last tone of the run, but it should not strain. If you strain to hold the belly out, it means you are holding your breath.

Because it is internal, it's hard to feel the movement of the diaphragm itself. The only part of your body you should feel moving is your upper abdominal region (above the navel), jumping out and in quickly as it is indirectly compressed by the moving diaphragm inside your rib cage. You can place your finger just below your breastbone to feel this movement.

On inhale, the diaphragm moves down. As it goes down, it pushes the upper abdomen out. On exhale in normal singing, the diaphragm and the upper abdominal muscles very slowly return to their starting positions. Only when the diaphragm relaxes completely does the upper abdomen move back into its normal position. In a staccato exercise like this one, the movement is faster because we're doing everything in rapid succession on purpose.

Don't squeeze the lower belly muscles; it actually fights the diaphragm's natural motion.

Keep the Throat Open

The vocal cords are very small. From front to back, they may only measure about 5/8 to 3/4 of an inch. Too much air pressure underneath can force them apart. Because of the pressure, you may reflexively feel the need to squeeze the throat so as not to lose too much at one time, which then forces you to push for the sound to come out.

If the throat closes, sound cannot flow freely and easily without discomfort. Problems with natural flow of air and pitch do not correct themselves if you are closing the throat to grab a pitch. Some singers do this to try to add more feeling to certain words. It's called a *glottal attack*. (The *glottis* is the opening between the vocal cords.) This method of singing, unless used only once in a while for a stylistic effect, can often lead to even more problems.

Check the Recording

If you can hear from listening back to a recording of what you have practiced that you were even slightly off pitch anywhere in this exercise, then you took in too much air and were forced to hold it for a second just before starting that first note (the 5). It only takes a second or less of holding in the air to close the throat. Hold your breath. Do you feel something inside your neck closing? If you've heard your first note falling flat of the pitch live or on tape, holding the breath may have been the culprit. However, don't over-intellectualize with the information you've been given. Instead, listen and evaluate the problem. Thought is in the evaluation, and the only thinking needed before starting once again.

Thought Is the Enemy of Action

Thinking too much while exercising or singing is crippling. Information will only take you so far when it comes to leaning how to sing correctly and protectively. Rather than the information you've accumulated in your mind, it is action that is needed. Feeling, watching, listening, and monitoring are all actions—things to *do*, not thoughts. Learning how to sing anything the way you desire comes from physically doing and can't be accomplished by only using information. Without the use of all your senses to experience the right way, the puzzle pieces of both intellectual and physical won't come together. Nothing will ever make sense to you.

Whatever thoughts you have should come during, or directly following, listening back to the tape to make an evaluation. No more thought is needed once you've diagnosed a problem (if there is one). The ability to determine wrong from right comes from listening as if this were a tape of another singer, and if possible, sympathetically feeling what happened on the tape. These actions alone help you to remember what to do just before you begin again. It is that simple. If it doesn't become that simple, you will continue to struggle through the exercises. Let go of what is rolling around in your head and listen to your sound not from within, but using your ears to hear it as others would. Closely observe things as you've been asked to observe. Learn to perceive through physical sensations, or you're very likely to never know what you're doing.

Listen for the Inhale

If you don't hear that tiny bit of inhale before each note, then it's wrong. Leaving out that inhale will cause problems you'll hear on the tape as: the voice breaking on the 5, a tone that isn't clear on each note, strain on the 5 the higher you go (which may also result in loss of pitch), and/ or bursting out of those little staccato sounds, which may also have made you dizzy.

Temporarily hesitating between notes can fool you into thinking you've inhaled correctly because you can hear, and even feel, a small break in the sound. It may have just been a glottal attack without an inhale. If you can't be sure there is an actual puff of air before each note, then listen for it on tape.

The AH Vowel

The shaping of vowels starts behind the back of the tongue and ends in the mouth. The HAH in the staccato exercise keeps the throat open. If your H starts right behind the back of the tongue, it will make it easy for sound to be exhaled without using the force of your breath. If you hear the word HUH (like the sound you'd make when catching a football) as you perform Exercise 4 or listening back to your tape, it's a sure sign of forced air. Stay on HAH, not HUH.

Sustaining the last note a bit longer than the rest will help you to hear, feel, and know whether the cords are controlling the flow of air. Besides helping the throat stay open, the AH in HAH also keeps the cords closer together. Allowing the AH to modify to UH lets the cords come apart so that too much air can escape. In the beginning of this training, you may not notice that HAH somehow modified to HUH unless you listen back to the tape. HUH can leave you feeling unable to prolong the last note of the run. If it feels uncontrollable, wavering, and unsteady, it's wrong. You will have to go back to the tape and listen for what happened. If you don't hear it right away, keep rewinding until you do.

Throughout this book, we'll use American English pronunciation for all words and phonetically-spelled syllables used for practice. Don't be afraid to consult a dictionary. Non-native English speakers—or those who just have an accent of some kind—may need to seek help from a dialect coach if they are in doubt about the correct pronunciation of these sounds as written.

V. Practicing the New Way

 **CD PRACTICE TRACK 7** • 54321 Men

 **CD TRACK 12** • 54321 Women

 **CD DEMO TRACK 18** • Legato 54321 on HAH

EXERCISE 5. LEGATO 54321 ON HAH

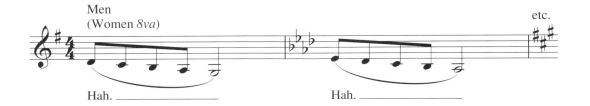

The term *legato* means a smooth, even sound with no noticeable interruption between notes. The same method of taking in a small amount of air that you used for the staccato exercise should be used for this one, but now you inhale just once at the beginning of each run. The H is only on the first note, and it should be produced behind the back of the tongue as before—not with the belly. The rest of the run is one continuous AH with changing pitch. The vowel should stay exactly the same throughout. Legato trains for the much-needed steady, flowing, fluid-like tones used when singing songs.

On all the legato exercises throughout this book, you will listen for the constant smooth stream of sound and a consistent vowel when performing the runs. If you can't feel or hear it as you go, you'll have to go back to the tape. The tape will not lie.

The Diaphragm Supports

With the above exercise, the only time you should have to pay attention to your body is if you feel yourself tightening anywhere, especially on the starting note of the run (scale degree 5) in each successively higher key. If you think the lower belly muscles have gotten involved by squeezing in to push the air up for sound, lightly place an index finger on that region and watch it. Is that section staying firm, or is it pushing inward and up on the exhale?

Only the upper abdomen between the sternum and the navel should exhibit any movement as the diaphragm performs its natural function. The upper abdomen expands on the inhale and stays firm throughout the run until you've finished the final tone. This is different from the staccato exercise, where this region moved rapidly out and in. The legato exercise is a bit less physically demanding as a result.

Let Go and Start!

To let go of any leftover breath you may be holding before beginning this exercise, simply relax your belly for a moment. Then, take in a bit of air like you did for the staccato exercise and quickly START! Don't hold the breath! Don't think! Just GO!

After you descend from the 5 through 4321, stay on the last note (the 1) a little longer than the others. It should all be smooth, but especially if the last note is steady and sustainable, you'll know your cords controlled the flow of air instead of you trying to control it with your body. If you feel tightness, if you start running out of air, or if you feel your abdominals moving inward any more than a very small amount before you finish a run, you will know it's wrong.

Make the Voice Your Student

With each new successively-higher key, repeat the same instructions. If at any time you feel tightness or hear a problem with your pitch or tone, replay your tape and listen closely to identify and fix problems before moving higher. Because we are working on developing correct habits for a stronger, freer voice, you'll need to keep reminding yourself that these exercises are not about identifying you as a good singer. They are all about retraining instincts that are in your way.

In this sense, the exercises will always be harder than singing. They'll act as an ever-constant challenge because it is only while exercising that you are allowed to strive for perfection. Why? Because you are in the process of breaking bad habits. Allowing them in, even the least bit, only continues to reinforce them.

When singing songs, you should not have to think about *any* of the things you practice in exercises. Rather, you should be focusing on articulation, placement, where to take breaths, the meaning of the words, and your art. It is the articulators and vowel shaping of words that create automatic correct placement and support. You must study and practice these things while vocalizing with exercises rather than *sound* for your desired result.

Natural Motions

When air is taken in correctly, upper abdominal and other muscles automatically spread out, or expand, at the front and sides. The back muscles also play a part in the expansion, but if you're focusing your attention on the upper abdominals, you don't need to worry about your back. In fact, you don't need to manipulate by straining or tightening any muscles to make correct expansion happen. The expansion should be a natural consequence of proper air intake. We will, however, later take steps to strengthen these muscles.

If the correct amount of air has been taken in, the diaphragm drops down a bit; the upper abdomen spreads in an outward motion to make room for air in the lungs. There is expansion around the waist (also called the *girth*). When the tones are in actual production, the diaphragm will slowly reverse its motion.

If you are trying to push for higher notes by constricting the lower belly muscles, sucking them in, and then thrusting the air up, this will push the diaphragm up resulting in the loss of its strength for support. Remember that the vocal cords have to control the flow of air or you won't be able to increase the strength, endurance, and power of your voice by using correct breathing technique.

The higher you go while performing any exercise, you should notice that the upper abdomen spreads out and expands even more for support, including the muscles that wrap around each side of the torso. However, the muscles below the belly button should still remain firm and unmoving.

After practicing the exercise in three or four successively-higher keys, think back on what you did and ask yourself how it felt. Did you feel any strain? If you don't know, listen to the tape. If you hear you've held the breath again, then you know old muscle sense-memory automatically kicked in. You'll have to do it again. Once you've determined the problem, it is in your diagnosis that you remind yourself what to do before starting again. Just start, and use your physical senses to pay attention. On these short run exercises, it's harder to feel some of these things than it is on the longer ones, making it essential to rewind the tape and record again and again until it's right.

Imitation

It can take a long time to recognize the feeling of tightening in an attempt to control air if this is how you've always tried to keep from running out. The habit could be so firmly ingrained that you don't know if you are doing it or not. Keep rewinding sections of tape until you are able to make a determination. After a while, if you find you are still unable to figure out what's going on, still not able to hear anything, then it's time to start imitating yourself.

This is something I do in lessons to show students what they're doing wrong. Imitate yourself and you'll detach your self-esteem from your voice. Imitation puts you in the position of teacher. To become that teacher and the voice your student, you have to be willing to make a complete fool out of yourself by sounding and looking ridiculous when doing it. Why be afraid to make fun of what you hear on tape? Imitation is simply exaggeration. You are the only one doing the imitating, so who cares?

When you go to imitate the tape, don't spend any time trying to figure out what you heard. The idea is to stop thinking altogether. Go directly for sound. If you over-analyze, you'll end up holding your breath before you even start, which only results in the repetition of the same old habit. There's no time for pause or hesitation if this method is to be of any benefit in determining a problem if there is one.

VI. Projecting a Resonant Tone

💿 **CD PRACTICE TRACK 7** • 54321 Men

💿 **CD TRACK 12** • 54321 Women

💿 **CD DEMO TRACK 19** • Staccato 54321 on MY

EXERCISE 6. STACCATO 54321 USING A CONSONANT WITH A DIPHTHONG: MY

Sections covering staccato exercises in this book always come first and contain more explanation than those covering legato. The quick-breath staccato we're using early on retrains the way you inhale and exhale. The legato exercises are the practical application and a good test of the skill learned in the staccato exercise using the same run.

With the addition of a consonant, you have more things to pay attention to when vocalizing. Although all sung tones are technically vowels, the proper execution of consonants is critically important. When singing songs, the consonants—not breath technique alone—become the facilitators for resonant tones. *Resonance* is reflection and amplification of sound by sympathetic vibration of bones—in this case the bones of the face. Properly executed consonants keep your tone strong and your voice powerful.

When singing, consonants can close the throat and prevent this resonance, especially if you are incorrectly pronouncing words by clenching the lower abdominal muscles or grabbing with muscles from inside the throat for an edgy sound. Methods like this are wrong because they keep the sound trapped in your body. We are going to learn to use only the proper *articulators* to pronounce consonants. The articulators are all located in the mouth. They are the *tongue, lips, teeth,* and *palate.*

THE FOUR ARTICULATORS

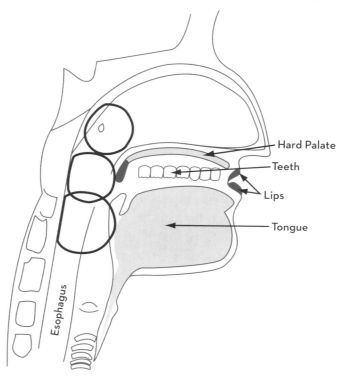

Hard Palate

Teeth

Lips

Tongue

Esophagus

Using an Articulator: The Lips

We'll start with the consonant M because it's one of the easier ones. The M pops off the lips alone as a short, light, sudden, and very quick action. Let me stress: the M should pop off the lips in an instant! The mouth should open immediately following that action as the vowel is produced.

If you keep the lips closed for any length of time to pronounce the M (as in a hum), you'll most likely find yourself grabbing with the inside of your gut. When that happens, the sound is trapped below, which will force you to use your body to push it up. If you find yourself the slightest bit flat on any of the pitches anywhere in the run, you grabbed with your abdominals.

PHARYNX AND MASK PLACEMENT
APPROXIMATION

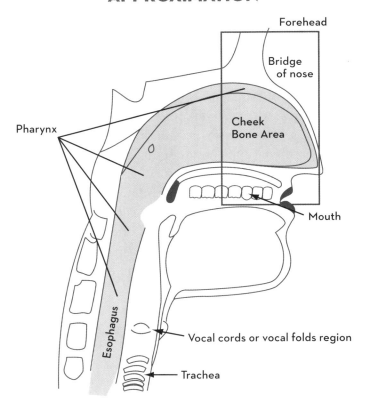

The Mask

To the M in this exercise we're adding a *diphthong*: a sound formed by two merged vowels, to create the word MY. The combination of the two vowels AH/EE helps keep the sound resonating in the mask. The *mask* is the part of the bone structure of the face that starts at mouth level, goes up across the cheekbones, and then extends up into the eyebrow and forehead area. If you visualize a costume ball mask, you'll get the picture.

A typical description of mask resonance might give you the false idea that it should be felt intensely. You may find yourself going after such a sensation by exerting pressure. This could force the sound into the nose rather than directly behind it, which is where it should be felt. If you find yourself sounding nasal, you may have been pushing air into your nose.

To stay resonating in the mask, you only need to be acoustically and physically sensing the lowest notes of your register (no matter how low they may be) vibrating at mouth level. If you can't hear and feel it at mouth level on your own, then use the tape recorder. When the mask is resonating, the tone is bright and unmuffled. If it is not, the vowel drifts into a dull UH, its tone is muffled, and it can be heard to drop below the chin if you listen closely.

Modifying MY to MUH can cause you to fall flat of the pitch. Repeat aloud the word MY, then MUH, again and again. Eventually you should not only hear but also feel the MUH as dropping out of the mouth area. Keep going back and forth between MY and MUH until you get the sensation. MUH is wrong in this exercise and will kill your mask placement. Learn how it feels when it is wrong, because then you can begin learning how to correct it.

The Pharynx

The *pharynx* is the tube that extends from the esophagus to the mouth and all the way up through the nose to its bridge. There are four parts of the pharynx: the *laryngeal pharynx*, the *oral pharynx*, the *upper pharynx*, and the *nasal pharynx*. The laryngeal and oral pharynges, often referred to as the "second mouth" of the singer, are chiefly responsible for shaping vowels and directing sound into the mask. When the sound and air come up through this tube without interference, resonance is created in the face, traveling into the sinus cavities. When it all functions correctly, it's like having your own internal amplifier.

PHARYNX — FACILITATES RESONATION
APPROXIMATION

Four sections of resonance — Laryngeal, upper, oral, nasal
Articulators — Tongue, teeth, lips, palate
Mask — mouth to bridge of nose and forehead
Voice Box — Vocal cords or vocal folds region

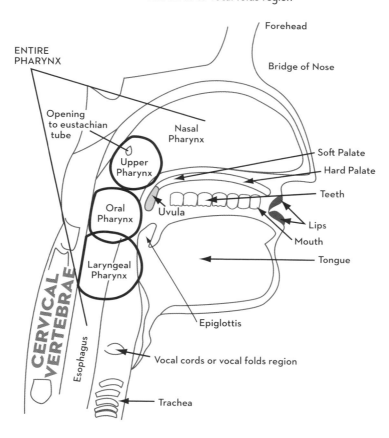

Pronouncing the Diphthong

Using a mirror, look at your mouth as you speak the word MY. Pop the M off the lips and immediately open the mouth for the diphthong. It should open at least an inch from the top of the lower lip to the bottom of the upper lip. Exaggerate the sound of the two vowels in the diphthong. Go from a pure AH to a pure EE. When pronouncing the AH-EE, the mouth should form a relaxed and open smile.

As you do this, ask yourself if you can physically sense the AH on top of the middle of the palate. If you can't yet, it's okay. You'll be able to feel this sensation when you get the hang of how to inhale the air for proper exhale with sound.

As you go higher with each successive key, focus a little more on the AH rather than the EE of the diphthong. This will help keep the mouth and the throat open. On the lowest note of each run, extend the EE. This pronunciation of going back to the EE helps keep the sound resonating in the mouth.

Keep the M Short

The higher you get with the top note in every new key, remain mindful of the fast-acting inhale just before the immediate articulation of the M popping off the lips alone. Singers have a tendency to forget about this as they continue moving forward with the exercise. If you feel your belly tighten before you finish the run, the M may have gotten stuck down there because you stayed on it too long and did not use the lips quickly enough to propel the vowel properly.

Again, if listening back to tape alone is not helping, go to imitation. You shouldn't be sucking in heaps of air just because there are no breaks with legato vocalises. The inhale should be the same, even when you begin practicing longer legato runs. Legato vocalises will help train you to sustain any note for as long as you wish in song. Of special note, the higher you get in pitch, the less air will be needed to get from start to finish of a run.

VII. Mask Placement Throughout the Range

CD PRACTICE TRACK 7 • 54321 Men

CD TRACK 12 • 54321 Women

CD DEMO TRACK 20 • Legato 54321 on MY

EXERCISE 7. LEGATO 54321 ON MY

This exercise starts with the same consonant, M, and has the same diphthong, AH-EE, but now we're doing it legato. Most of the legato exercises are an opportunity to find out if you are successfully retraining yourself to take in the right amount of air before exhaling for sound. Because legato has no breaks in between notes, the run should be smooth and fluid. The focus is on the act of listening to the sound as others hear it (not from inside your head).

If the sound becomes unsteady, you're blowing out too much air while executing the run. Holding the breath before you start the first note (the 5) makes you feel as if you are going to have to thrust some air up to exhale for sound. If that's happening, you took in too much air, too heavily and too deeply. The result is collapse of diaphragmatic support and cords at the same time.

Legato vocalises are not nearly as physical in action as are staccato ones. The first inhale is the same as in the staccato exercise: short, light, and very quick. There will be one M popping off the lips, followed by an extended AH that slowly modifies to EE by the last note of the run. Sustain the low note of each run (the 1) like you did on the staccato version. This ensures the cords are controlling the flow of air.

Vowel Shaping for MY

Make sure your MY includes the complete diphthong and not just MAH. MY (MAH-EE) and MAH are two distinctly different sensations. Each takes on a different direction of air when pronounced. Repeat the two words aloud until you feel the MAH as a vertical sensation. The AH vowel is felt on the middle of the palate. The EE in MAH-EE takes your voice to a horizontal sensation across the mask.

Begin morphing into the EE by the 3rd note of the run to keep the later notes from dropping out of the mouth area. If you feel the last note of a run has dropped some of its focused intensity (we call it *edge*) and sounds airy, lean more toward the EE on the diphthong than the AH. This should keep the resonance at mouth level. On the other extreme, don't morph into EE too quickly, or you may begin to lose your open throat, since EE has such a horizontal feel to it (much more than that of other vowels).

If you are questioning anything, always go back to your tape. Sometimes you may find yourself having to rewind only one section several times before your acoustical senses accurately perceive the sounds as we hear them. It's easy to think you have the hang of something just because you want to get on with it. This impatience will only keep reinforcing what still remains incorrect. It's best to go back and rewind that tape as many times as needed in order to determine if it has been executed correctly.

Moving Through the Registers

Many singers find their lowest notes are not as strong as they should be. Learning how to keep these notes resonating in the mouth by focusing on that smile of the diphthong, or an exaggeration of it, strengthens the muscle groups controlling the vocal cords by helping them to maintain their stretch for pitch. Again, make sure you do not allow the diaphragm to relax before you have reached the **end** of the last note of the run. It must remain just as firm, if not firmer, as you come down to that last note.

When pronouncing the AH-EE diphthong, the smile intensifies when leaning toward the EE. A smile on the outside helps lift the soft palate arches on the inside. (The soft palate begins where the hard palate ends. Slide your tongue backwards along the roof of your mouth and you will feel it). You can't lift them voluntarily, but raising the soft palate arches with proper vowel shaping will help keep the throat open. Open throats help keep the cords stretching from front to back for pitch. All things working together as a single unit makes mask placement and resonance easy to sustain.

The middle range of notes is felt behind the nose and/or directly behind and against the cheekbones. If it moves further back on the palate, it may sound trapped when you play back the recording. If that is what you hear, you will know to think about keeping the shape of those vowel sounds and not allowing them to modify before you try once again.

The upper middle area of the voice is felt at the bridge of the nose, while the highest notes of a range should be felt directly behind or above the eyebrows. If you have a particularly high register, you will probably feel that resonance going up into the forehead.

Common Placement Terms

If your sound is too nasal, an instructor might say you've forced the air and sound straight into the nose and ask you to correct it. On the other hand, when sound is too far back in the throat, or trapped, the instructor may ask you to bring the sound "more forward." *More forward* is just another way of telling you to place the sound in the mask: those resonating cavities of the face.

Good Placement Comes from Correct Breathing

Surprisingly, sound resonating at the front of the face is an end result of properly inhaled breath. Proper inhalation creates correct tonal placement automatically, because it keeps the diaphragm doing its sole job of supporting the vocal mechanism, where the vocal cords produce sound, the pharynx and mouth shape a vowel, and the articulators create consonants. If the diaphragm or abdominal muscles get involved in grabbing consonants or pushing vowels for placement, the system is out of order, and the placement will be wrong.

VIII. Self-Diagnosis

As you start to work your voice on any given day, it will be affected by everything you feel, think, do, or eat. If you feel happy, you'll probably have a good singing day. If you're depressed, it may be more difficult to sing because you won't feel like it. Your voice can be affected by foods you might be allergic to and don't know about, or foods that cause acid reflux. Allergies or acid reflux can create swelling and mucus, as do drugs, alcohol, and smoking of any kind.

If you are tired, your subconscious mind may tell you there isn't enough physical energy to give to your performance. Before you know it, incorrect habits start creeping back in as you try to gain the strength and power you think is missing. This will especially be true as you try to reach the higher notes in your songs.

However, thrusting and pushing up with air will not give you the power you seek. In fact, this action will initially close the throat. In response to excess air pressure, the cords slam shut to keep it from escaping all at once. Intensity of sound does not come from air alone. It comes from the strength and support of the diaphragm and its surrounding muscles, and strength of the muscle groups that control the stretch of the cords. Take stock of how you feel before starting to warm up and sing every day. If you feel tired, apathetic, or ill, it's even more important to focus on singing with good technique.

Not Working?

When practicing Exercises 6 and 7, never assume you have pronounced MY correctly throughout the run. It might be so on the first couple of notes, but many times MY won't stay on MY, even if you think it has. Listening back to the tape is the only way to be sure it didn't modify. Old sense-memory has a way of waiting in the wings so it can kick in. It likes to fight with you, so don't drift off somewhere in your head thinking about anything other than getting the pronunciation right.

During the course of practice, you may find out that your diaphragmatic region of muscle groups is weak and not performing its natural expansion. This can be especially true if you've been habitually using the lower belly muscles to push up for sound. Though it is true that the belly muscles come out at the start of initial inhale, after that, those muscles should remain firm and unmoving.

After much continued practice with still no success, **drastic measures may be required** to fix a persistent habit. It might be necessary to give an instruction that's normally incorrect or opposite to one usually given.

Problem 1: Still Using Belly Muscles

For example, if you've been singing by sucking and squeezing in that belly to push up the air for sound and cannot stop, you may have to think about totally dumping those muscles so the diaphragm can start working, developing, and strengthening. You also may find that monitoring this action by lightly placing your index finger on the belly button or just below will help. As you begin exercising, literally look down at your belly where your finger is and watch with your own eyes to see if your belly is punching in, then up, rather than the diaphragm doing its job by spreading out and expanding. Dump those belly muscles and see if you can feel the upper abdomen working more.

There have been times when I've needed to direct a singer back to the quick and fast dog pant action. Then, on exhale, I told them to literally **blow** the air out on the staccato MY just to get them to feel the breath coming out.

Problem 2: Still Too Nasal

If sound remains too nasal no matter how many times you try to get it out of the nose, try to think of placing the sound further back—straight up or vertical—and sense the resonance hitting the middle of the palate and above. For some reason, it helps the nasal singer place the voice directly behind the nose where it should be.

Problem 3: Still Trapped

If your sound is too far back, you may have to think about going straight into the nose. This helps a singer with this problem place the resonance behind the nose and in the mask, rather than staying trapped at the back of the mouth.

Nasal sounds, sound dropping out or down, and/or sound falling backwards should all be options for stylistic effect and not your only choice. Listen to the tape to identify when you're making these sounds.

Steady Volume

Do not start getting louder and louder on the 5 the higher you get with each new successive set of notes. If you start getting louder or feeling strain, you are pushing up the air by punching in with the belly muscles. This strain alone can result in falling short of the pitch.

Old muscle sense-memory is often so strong that no matter how many times you remind yourself of what to do, you won't be able to do it. However, after a bit of practice, you will learn how it feels to have produced tones incorrectly and old habits will start feeling uncomfortable enough for you to want to reverse them.

When you get to the point that you are able to feel when you have performed something wrong, then you are halfway through the process of retraining how to take in the air. Until you get to this point, you cannot move into learning how to correct it.

If you are having a problem with any single one of the runs, then stop and spend some time in that area. Re-work the area until you get it right. Any amount of time spent working in one area will help the entire range of your voice because you are working at changing a habit.

Work only one troublesome area for a while, and then test your work by going to an easier register. Even if you didn't get it right all the time in that one problem area, you should feel improvement in the easier areas.

Practice Takes Patience

New ways of doing things seem harder than the old. Frustration comes from not knowing what makes it right when it's right and how to make sure you do it the same way next time. It is the transition from wrong to right, the in-between place of the unknown until the known finally manifests, that gets so frustrating.

If you find yourself getting angry, it can affect your self-esteem so badly that you feel you'll never learn how to sing with ease. There may even come a time when you feel like throwing your tape out the window and giving up completely. If you find yourself getting too frustrated, stop. Do something else for a while and tackle it again later, or the next day. Anger will only set you up to continue to reinforce incorrect habits.

No matter what, never give up. If you really want to become a professional singer and save your voice from injury as you journey upward and onward, you must learn patience. Commit to the idea that this is a **process**, a continuing development involving many steps and changes.

Technical exercising sometimes frightens singers into thinking they will lose their emotional artistry and style. I urge you to trust that this book will teach how to transfer new habits to songs with any style and emotional content you want. However, practice like this is necessary if new habits are to become second nature.

IX. Strengthening the Diaphragm and Related Muscles

How Respiratory Muscles Can Stay Weak

If you take in too much air and push it out for sound, then you probably have weak diaphragmatic, upper abdominal, and back muscles. Compensation for the weakness will have you resorting to the use of lower belly and neck muscles. Over time, the misuse will become a habit, and you'll engage these muscles reflexively to sing. Everything below the belly button will most likely feel heavily at work while the diaphragm seems to be taking a nap. Our next exercises will use a simple piece of equipment to speed up the development of the muscles, as you continue to work on correct breathing habits.

But First, My Apologies

Before we begin tackling this next exercise, I must apologize to all the instructors I made fun of who used props like bricks, books, or weights to strengthen the diaphragm. Their students would come to me and demonstrate by placing the prop just on top of the navel and pumping their lower abdominals in and out. Every time I watched a student show me what they thought they'd been taught, I'd think, "What is this? P.E.?" A few years later, I found that, when properly done, it's actually quite similar to taking the diaphragm to the gym.

Five to ten years ago, all I knew was that abdominal expansion for support of the diaphragm was supposed to be a natural response to an inhalation. I didn't have the words to explain how to engage the diaphragm properly. I only knew you weren't supposed to suck in air or push it out with those low belly muscles, and I stopped my students from doing it. I moved their focus away from the diaphragm and found other methods that proved to help hundreds of people—especially the singers who came to me with pitch problems, loss of range, hoarseness, and nodes. All of them improved, and many had their damages heal. Exceptions were those that had long-term damage such as paralysis of one or both vocal cords, or conditions requiring surgery such as polyps and cysts. After their operations, even these voices could come back to me and be successfully rehabilitated.

I continued to hear confusion and arguments among students and other instructors about how to engage the diaphragm over the years, so I made this a focus of my continued research into the voice. Finally it occurred to me: maybe it isn't that the other teachers are wrong. Maybe the students are misperceiving the idea because of the words used to describe what they were supposed to be doing. Rather than a real disagreement, that would be a semantic problem.

At the back of this book is a glossary of dictionary-defined terms teachers use for instruction. Most of us are trying to teach the same things to all singers, but we all use different words to describe them. When looking up many terms myself, I was shocked by some of their true meanings. I think you will be too, so don't skip the glossary. Use it. I'm hoping that many students and teachers will see why, in reality, correct perception all comes down to the true meaning of a word.

🖸 **CD PRACTICE TRACK 7** • 54321 Men

🖸 **CD TRACK 12** • 54321 Women

🖸 **CD DEMO TRACK 21** • Staccato with Prop 1234 54321 on MEE

EXERCISE 8. USE OF PROP ON STACCATO 1234 54321 WITH CONSONANT AND VOWEL: MEE

If you resort to tightening and blowing to try to reach notes with power, you can pretty much bank on the fact that the diaphragmatic muscles, upper abdominals, and supporting back muscles aren't working well (if they're working at all). The prop helps strengthen these muscles and, when used the right way, it reinforces the action of correct intake of air before exhaling with sound. Any singer can benefit from this work.

My prop of personal choice is a twelve-pound athletic ball. (Talk about a work out!) These balls can be found at any sports shop. The one I have is made by Everlast and cost about $40.00. I like this ball because it has built-in handles on each side that make it easy to hold it up on the upper abdominal area and perform exercises while standing. If you can't get a ball like this, you can try a heavy book. The mass of the prop makes it easier to hold it steady. You're not going to be tossing it around like a boxer in training.

How to Use the Prop

Stand up and hold the ball directly on the soft muscle of the upper abdomen. The two sides of your ribcage form a large upside-down V that surround the area. Do not place the ball down on the stomach region.

This will be just as much a visual exercise as it is physical. Watch closely throughout the exercise to make sure you're following the instructions. As you first inhale, the abdomen should expand and move the ball out about a quarter of an inch. This will be the place where you should hold the ball throughout the rest of the run. As you sing the first staccato tone, the upper abdomen moves away from the ball. With each successive inhalation, the upper abdomen should spread out against the ball again.

As in the previous exercises, you will inhale only a small puff of air before each note, and you will not stop to hold your breath. Listen for inhalation.

Don't pump the ball in and out with your arms. It should stay still while the diaphragm spreads out against it. If your arms move, then you're using the ball to push in the diaphragm rather than using the diaphragm to spread out against the ball.

Should you notice that your upper abdomen has stopped spreading out against the ball and remains unmoving, or that the staccato notes seem to be getting harder and harder to perform, you're holding your breath before you inhale. It's also possible that you're not really inhaling that little puff of air for each note.

Since this exercise is longer than the previous ones, it will give you the opportunity to find out if you can keep singing without closing the throat anywhere throughout the run. It is a vocalise that not only continues training you how to take in air properly, but also helps strengthen and build up the diaphragmatic muscles even more.

Vowel Shaping for MEE

Whenever possible, make use of consonants to help achieve mask placement. Later vocalises in this book will use other consonants, continuing to train the use of the articulators for this purpose. For places in songs where you sing vowels with no consonants—"oohs" or "ahhs," for example—you have to rely on proper breathing technique and shaping of the vowels for directing your placement into the mask. This particular exercise, however, continues with popping the M off the lips for mask placement while we focus on breathing and vowel shaping.

You need to keep similar placement for mask resonance on all vowels, so this exercise moves us on to a new one: EE. For the word MEE, we want to keep the same placement we had on MY. The mouth is a little less open on MEE than it was for the EE part of MY. On MEE, you'll also feel the middle of the tongue rise up slightly more than it does on MY. Keep switching back and forth between the two spoken words, MAH-EE and MEE, until you feel the differences in the mouth shape and the tongue position.

The resonance on EE is felt in the mouth directly behind the upper front teeth. When it is right, you may feel as though your front teeth are buzzing a little. You'll need to focus on sensation in this area if you notice your lowest notes start to become weak, sound airy, and drop down below mouth level. The resistance that one feels from tone hitting the bones of the face is like a brace that works in cooperation with the diaphragm. Notice I said this a feeling and not a physical reality. On a mechanical level, the diaphragm is only providing a steady supply of air pressure in the exact amount needed by the vocal cords.

A Round Trip from 1 to 1

When starting this exercise, remember where you felt the placement in the mask on the first note of the run. On descent, you will come back to that exact same placement on the final note of the run, because it is the same pitch. This helps sense-memorize its position and strengthen those notes.

If careful listening to the tape shows you are not pronouncing a true EE in the low-to-lower middle registers, you'll have to practice that area until you can hear (and feel) the placement landing in the mouth just behind the teeth, with resonance and edge. It should not be airy as you reach your lowest notes. If it is, you are relaxing all the muscles needed for support before you've actually finished the last note.

Modifying EE to IH

As you get into the upper middle and high registers, you'll find that modifying the highest note (the 5 of the key) to IH (as in the word *hit*) will help keep the throat open. At this point, a true EE can become so horizontal in sensation that it closes the throat. Try a true EE on a very high note and you will feel how hard it is to produce. Modify MEE to MIH on those high notes, and you will feel how much easier it is.

As you return to lower keys, you can begin pronouncing a true EE again. Remember to keep the EE at mouth level for edge and mask placement. Check the tape. If the top note of any run sounds strained, you can modify the EE of that note more to IH and try again. If the bottom note loses edge and sounds airy, make sure you're going back to a true EE as you come back down the scale. If you're still not getting it, try a very exaggerated smile while singing MEE on those lowest notes.

As with MY, listen to the tape to make sure your MEE doesn't drift into a MUH. If it does, again, it means you relaxed your supporting muscles before you finished the last note. You'll know it if the last note sounds considerably weaker than all the other pitches.

Maintain Steady Loudness

When practicing Exercise 8, make sure each staccato note stays at the same level of loudness within a run. If you're increasing your power through correct diaphragmatic support and resonance, the sound volume should stay the same. Though there will be some volume changes as you move through your entire range, if you are getting louder on the higher notes within one single scale, something is amiss. It means you're likely pushing more air, and you'll have to go back to a lower volume overall and reassess your technique.

You only begin boosting the strength and power of your voice when you start becoming more familiar with new feelings and ways of doing things. Using the force of your air alone won't work. If you can sustain the last note in each successive key with a focused intensity at least half the time, then you can move on to the legato exercise in the next chapter and try adding more weight and power to it in the same way.

X. Getting the Diaphragm, Vocal Cords, and Mask Working Together

When you learn the natural action of air intake and exhaling with sound, the diaphragmatic muscle groups will gradually be strengthened. They will start to act as a brace for the entire instrument. The stronger the brace, the easier it is to add intensity, power, and resonance.

Support of the diaphragmatic region of muscles, the weight and stretch of the cord, and mask placement all act as bracing tension for one another.

Powerful and strong (or not), all placement in the mask should feel relatively the same. When the support of the diaphragm is increased to boost the power, you'll feel your upper abdomen expand a little more, and the sensations behind the cheekbones will slightly increase. Overemphasis on the mask in lessons can lead students to think they must blow their faces off to feel an intense vibration.

CD PRACTICE TRACK 8 • 123454321 Men

CD TRACK 13 • 123454321 Women

CD DEMO TRACK 22 • Legato with Prop 123454321 on MEE

EXERCISE 9. USE OF PROP ON LEGATO 123454321 WITH CONSONANT AND VOWEL: MEE

Place your athletic ball or other prop on the upper abdomen below the ribs, just as you did for the staccato. This time you will be watching closely to make sure the abdomen expands against the ball and stays firmly against that ball all the way through the run. Again, do not move the prop in and out by punching it in with your arms and pushing it out with the belly. That prop should be held firm and unmoving after you have started the run.

Before each scale, there should be a quick inhalation just as you used on the staccato exercise, as if you've been suddenly startled by something. If the inhalation is correct, the throat will not squeeze shut.

The legato vocalise is much more like singing phrases in songs, unless you are breaking up words with staccato phrasing for a stylistic effect. As you perform each successive iteration, you have to be listening objectively to hear if the run comes out as a steady stream. If the sound wavers anywhere during the run, it means too much air was taken in. Again, this will make it difficult for the cords to compress and control the flow. Rather, the belly will instinctively hold in the air as an automatic response to keep it from being released too fast.

Low Register Mouth Placement

As with the staccato M on MEE, that M must pop off the lips quickly as they immediately open. Keep the same wide smiling EE at mouth level for mask placement in low registers. Try to sense-memorize the placement of the first note so you can go back to it at the end of the run. Extend the last note of the run to give yourself time to see whether you were able to return to the initial placement. If you're not sure, listen to the tape—repeatedly, if necessary.

Watch the prop closely to make sure the diaphragm is spreading out against it. As you begin working in the lower register, you need to make sure the upper abdomen is spread and the cords are engaged, even though it won't be as obvious as it is in the higher ranges. The lower register is your foundation, and if it is not strong, you will not be able to sustain higher pitches.

Upper Register Vowel Modification

As the exercise ascends to higher keys, you'll need to start vowel modification from EE to IH on the higher notes. It's the only way the throat will stay open. Start modifying the vowel as soon as you suspect your throat may close on the next note. This means, for upper-middle register runs, you will only have to modify the highest note (scale degree 5). This will vary from person to person, so I can't say exactly where it will be for you. As you come back down that scale run, return to EE on the very next pitch: scale degree 4. As you perform higher runs, the modification to IH will come earlier until, at the highest part of your range, you're forced to pronounce the word as MIH all the way through the run in order to keep your throat open. Here you're also developing the sensitivity needed to correctly bridge your registers, which we'll be covering more deeply in Chapter XIII.

Practice at a Moderate Volume

When vocalizing in exercise, it's unnecessary and counterproductive to practice at full-tilt loudness. You're focusing on your breathing—not sonic volume. You must work without complaint about how it sounds to you. Complaining about your sound means you are not paying attention to the correctness of the exercise.

Trust that loudness will increase with practice. Take the analogy of going to the gym. Building up muscles doesn't happen overnight. One must practice religiously, with correct technique, for things to change. Apply the same idea to any part of the voice that needs work. If you give the voice three to five days per week of focused practice and repetition, then in about six weeks you can expect noticeable improvement in all areas with regard to singing.

Getting the hang of these new ideas takes patience. With patience, you'll be able to work up to a much stronger sound with less difficulty and be less likely to push, hold your breath, or stay locked into whatever incorrect habits you've had.

Give yourself time to contemplate some of these ideas before you sit down to practice. You'd be surprised what a little time off can do for your instrument just because you gave things some subconscious thought. Time away allows the mind to process what couldn't be physically understood before you took a break. Once you resume practicing, you may notice that, even though you didn't actively vocalize, some things have automatically fallen into place. If you have vocal problems, you can't just keep manipulating unnecessary muscle groups for loudness expecting different results.

> To be sure you're performing any diaphragmatic and upper abdominal exercises correctly, try placing your hands on your belly below the navel. This area should come out when you inhale, then remain completely unmoving throughout the rest of the exercise until you finally relax well after the last note is done. If you feel that part of your belly squeezing in or pushing up, then it is not allowing the diaphragm to do its job. Instead it's pushing up on it, which collapses the support. Feel that lower belly with your hands as you do an exercise and you'll know.

Keep the Spread

To make sure the diaphragm does not collapse too soon, focus on spreading the upper abdomen out even more the higher you go. This means you will have to exert some pressure behind it—without holding the breath—to try to get it to expand. Keep that little bit of extra firmness as you come back down, until you get past your middle register.

Upon descent to lower keys, the spread of the upper abdomen should still be maintained to avoid collapse of the diaphragm, but it doesn't necessarily require that little bit of extra pressure we used in the higher keys. If you don't have an instructor, it is especially true that you are responsible for determining the right amount of pressure for bracing support throughout your entire range, without burdening the vocal cords with extra work to hold the air back.

It is in learning how to use the diaphragm and building up this muscle region that you gain control, bridge your registers, and strengthen the cords. Along with the mask placement that comes from correct articulation of consonants, the developed breath-control mechanism will give you more powerful tones.

> When you can't get the diaphragm and the voice to perform the way you have been instructed, it can get frustrating, and maybe even make you angry. Redirect these feelings into challenging yourself. Compete with the voice on the tape as if it were someone else. This separates your self-esteem from the way you judge your sound. You might find you enjoy practice more this way. Make the decision to win, and it is only a matter of time. At some point, your voice will not be able to fight your will.

XI. Vocal Cord Function

There is no new exercise for this chapter. We'll take some time to study the most delicate part of the mechanism, the vocal cords, and continue practicing Exercises 6, 7, 8, and 9, using the prop. You will exert the same amount of pressure behind the abdominals throughout the middle and upper registers. This will keep those muscles firmly against the prop. Do not allow the diaphragm to relax until you have completely finished the last note of each run. Diaphragmatic support throughout the entire range is needed to keep the cords engaged and the sound properly placed in the mask. If it's not there, the sound drops out, becomes airy, and loses its edge, because the cords have collapsed.

The Cords

The vocal cords' function should be similar to that of the two reeds of an oboe or bassoon vibrating together without strain, but with no extra air leaking through. Your goal is to get the two cords (or *folds*) to come together and sound as if they are one. If there is excessive contact between them in their vibrational cycles, the tone will be shrill. On the other extreme, if there is too much space between them, you'll hear breathiness in the tone. There is a sweet spot between the two extremes we refer to as correct cord engagement where they barely make contact. It is here you'll feel mask resonance happening most, and the tone will be powerful and smooth with a bright edge.

Stylistic Effects

You can take the edge away from your voice or exaggerate it for stylistic effect in song, but this should be a conscious decision made after correct engagement is an established habit. If taking edge out is your habit, it will keep your entire range weak. If exaggerating the edge is your habit, you will get nodes or polyps on your cords because of how tightly together you are closing them; it's just a matter of time.

A clean voice should be in place before you start adding effects of any kind. Each effect has technical requirements to master so that you don't hurt your voice while performing it. These should be learned from a qualified instructor who specializes in the style you want, whether it's breathiness for R&B sounds, raspiness and screaming for hard rock, or "death grunting" for extreme metal.

In the age of the internet, you can reach a teacher who's willing to help you from thousands of miles away through online lessons using voice-over-internet protocol. Some specialists I recommend are Melissa Cross, Tita Hutchison, Robert Lunte, and Jaime Vendera.

"Engage the Cords" Does Not Mean "Squeeze the Neck"

Don't try to cram the cords together by squeezing the neck muscles. If they are doing all the work to raise the pitch, it may give you the mistaken idea that the cords have come together. The throat will be drastically reduced in diameter, but the cords will not engage, and the tone will suffer. You could see this on a laryngoscope. If youtube.com is still in operation when you get this book, it would be a good idea to look at video clips tagged as "laryngoscopy." It is more likely you will find clips showing bad technique rather than good, because these are the people that wind up in a doctor's office.

With a neck-squeezing problem, by the time you get to the end of a run you'll feel like you have no air left. This will have you trying to eke out the last little bit just to finish the last note.

Avoiding Injury

If you are reluctant to engage your cords fully the higher you go because you're afraid of injury, you will hear breathy high notes. These will (and I'm sorry to sound like a broken record here) prevent the cords from compressing and controlling the flow of air. Bracing for the column of air doesn't just come from support of the diaphragm. It also comes from engaging and using your cords. If you don't use the cords to hit pitches, and instead try to reach them with increased air pressure, you are more likely to create the damage you fear. In other words, the instructions for correct phonation also protect the voice.

The Science of the Vocal Cords

VOCAL CORD OPEN FOR INHALATION

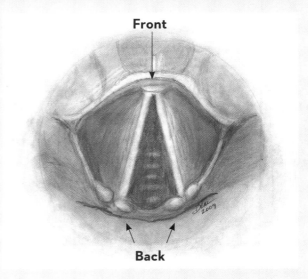

Pitch is determined by the stretch of the vocal cords. The lower the note, the looser the cords, and the bigger the opening between them. The higher the note, the more stretched the cords, and the smaller the opening between them. When a singer has developed good technique and strengthened the entire mechanism from top to bottom, the cords come together, rapidly (but gently) cycling into contact and then apart to produce a sound wave.

In the lower register, the entire cord structure is involved in vibration. The cords are loose and vibrate at low frequencies to produce low pitches. Somewhere in this lower register they produce your loudest sound, provided that the larynx is not dropped out of optimal position.

To sing higher pitches, the cords start getting stretched to a state of higher tension as they are pulled upon at their point of attachment to the *arytenoid cartilage* in the back of the larynx. The cords are drawn into a faster and smaller cycle as a result of this stretch.

Middle register notes lose some of the weight and heaviness of sound that the lower register had. The middle of either vocal cord structure (called the *vocalis muscles*) and their inner edges (the *vocal ligaments*) still vibrate, but the outer areas become less involved. This is why the sound starts to thin—but you can still retain a chest-like sound if you're maintaining proper support.

The cords stretch back the farthest in the upper register. Similar to a rubber band, the more stretched the vocal ligaments, the higher the pitch. In this register, the inner edge is vibrating, while the middle and outer parts of the cords aren't vibrating nearly as much. Because of this, the highest of your range is the register that loses the most weight, and sound is at its thinnest. Nonetheless, with increased support of the diaphragmatic muscles, this register too can retain some of that chest-like sound.

Speech Pathology

When a voice has been injured, the singer should seek out a reputable laryngologist for help. After treatment, surgery, or vocal rest, those doctors may suggest the services of a good speech pathologist to help repair the cords and teach how to prevent injury to the cords from occurring again.

Speech pathology and therapy are branches of medicine that deal with finding and correcting the cause of an injury to any part of the vocal mechanism, when the cause is abnormal pronunciation and variation of sounds. These specialists train people to speak properly by using the articulators to pronounce consonants and the laryngeal and oral pharynges to correctly shape vowels. The best are often skilled enough to also teach how to transfer the skills over to singing. There are some singers who have learned more from speech therapy than from any singing instructor. Learning how to pronounce consonants and vowels properly is essential to the preservation of your instrument.

XII. Isolation Exercises for Applied Technique

Correct use of the articulators to pronounce consonants is also (as we know) how we keep mask resonance. Combine this with correct vowel shaping and diaphragmatic support, and we have the elements of a foundation for proper technique. These elements must be practiced extensively using more of the possible consonants and vowels in the English language besides the ones we've used already in the book.

In these next three chapters, we'll learn three more vocalises that can be used with any consonants and vowels on which you need to refine your technique. Playing around with different combinations of consonants and vowels in these exercises will give you an idea of what might need practice before singing. Conversely, when singing a song, you may notice that a particular combination of sounds is giving you trouble, and you'll want to apply one or more of these exercises to it.

The three new exercises are:

1.) 1353 54321, an ascending major triad arpeggio that repeats the 3rd before descending the major scale from the 5.

2.) 135 8 531, an ascending and descending major triad arpeggio that includes the root an octave higher.

3.) 1-54321, a *portamento* (or glide) from the initial root to the 5th, followed by descending scale steps.

There are hundreds of exercises available on CD as part of book packages on the market. I encourage every singer to use any exercise they want to practice the concepts laid out in this book and to apply these principles to any exercise(s) they may be already using. Some exercises I found extremely helpful for my own practice are on the CDs for Seth Riggs's *Singing with the Stars* and Anne Peckham's *The Contemporary Singer*.

Though you may practice any consonant or vowel combination that you need, in this book we will not address all possible consonants and every diphthong in the English language. Instead, I've chosen only a few consonants to pronounce when singing. These are *hard consonants*, which means they naturally stop the flow of air.

B, a hard G as in good, K, M, N, and P.

These are the vowel sounds we'll use; they include four basic vowels and two diphthongs.

AH (as in the word *father*),

EE (as in the word *bee*),

OH (as in the word *ghost*),

OO (as in the word *noose*).

the diphthong AH-EE (as in the word *my*),

the diphthong EH-EE (as in the word *pay*).

Again, once you've gotten used to the exercises, you can use them on any vowel combination you need to refine—for example, OH-EE as in *toy*.

Our CD examples start with P and OH.

CD PRACTICE TRACK 9 • 1353 54321 Men

CD PRACTICE TRACK 14 • 1353 54321 Women

CD DEMO TRACK 23 • POs with Initial Inhale Only on 1353 54321

EXERCISE 10. POS WITH INITIAL INHALE ONLY ON 1353 54321

Sing a PO on each pitch, taking in a little bit of air before the first note of the run only. Again, use the lips only for the Ps. This exercise is performed all in one breath. Though you will feel and hear tiny stops between each PO, these are created by the articulation of the consonant, which stops the flow of air.

A Reminder

All consonants are articulated by using the lips, tongue, palate, and teeth only!

CD PRACTICE TRACK 9 • 1353 54321 Men

CD PRACTICE TRACK 14 • 1353 54321 Women

CD DEMO TRACK 24 • Arpeggio and Scale 1353 5432 1 with POs

EXERCISE 11. COMBINED ARPEGGIO AND SCALE 1353 5432 1 WITH POS

Here we practice POs and a legato run within the same exercise. Take in one small breath before singing the entire run. First sing 1353 (PO, PO, PO, PO). The hard consonant P will create small breaks in the sound. The second time you reach the 5th degree, sing PO but descend without any breaks on the vowel sound O alone through 54321. As you work this exercise into the upper middle register, do not start pushing up the air you think is needed for a loud and powerful sound. That sound is created with the proper support of the diaphragm, placement, and resonance—not pushing and yelling.

If you're articulating the P with the lips alone, you'll feel the vowel sound resonating in the mask. The cords should not break or blow apart anywhere during the course of this vocalise. If they do, you're trying to pull the sound and air into the mask by squeezing in and pushing up with your lower belly muscles.

You can change the vowel using this same consonant to create more monosyllabic building blocks for singing, e.g., PEH-EE (as in the word *pay*), PEE, PAH/EE (as in the word *pie*), or POO. You can also change the consonant and vowel and combine them into one exercise, e.g., PAY PAY PAY PAY BO BO BO BO BO (1353 54321). Don't forget the proper quick inhalation on the first note, and start the first note without holding the breath. Try it also staccato with an inhalation before each note.

As another example (chosen at random), try combining KAI and KEE, using KAI on the first half and switching to KEE for the descending scale. Inhale only before the first note to feel how the K stops the flow of air by itself. Remember to place your EEs with an open smile.

XIII. Bridging the Registers

If you've been squeezing your neck muscles to get through the middle or upper middle register, the transition between your registers (the *passagio*) is not bridged correctly. It may not be noticeable to your audience because of how good you've gotten at hiding it. If you are still feeling the glitch, it will continually undermine your self-esteem as a singer no matter how great everyone claims you are.

Often just learning how to take in exactly enough air for sound puts your diaphragm in the correct position, giving the laryngeal muscle groups that control the vocal cords the opportunity to develop the stretch needed for the voice to start bridging on its own. This could take from a year for a beginner to less than six months for an experienced singer. Instead of tensing up and forcing your way through the notes in this area, you're going to be extra vigilant about doing the exact opposite, concentrating on the things you've been doing thus far.

> All vocal problems come down to incorrect breath technique. The only exceptions are acid reflux and damage from drugs, alcohol, and smoking. If you don't change how heavily and deeply you take in your air, you will continue to feel discomfort, lack confidence, and at some point, might even create damage from vocal cord abuse. It's the nature of the instrument. Most wind instruments require light steady breath pressure; overblowing them creates nothing but squeaks and squawks.

Learning to bridge properly can take more time than you'd like. Year after year of ingrained instinctive actions create habits and conditions that interfere with bridging. Even if you are not aware of the habits, your body remembers them.

Having the intellectual information alone is not enough to control habits and develop diaphragm and vocal cord strength and flexibility. It takes repetitive practice with feeling the physical before you begin correcting. I will say this, though: I never believed in "magical voice fixes" before I stumbled across this universal problem with the breath. It does take time to retrain, but it doesn't take nearly as long as anything else I've ever tried to whip a voice into shape. In that sense, it **is** magical. With the guidance of a good instructor, you can start experiencing it from the first lesson.

Gaining control of your instrument buys you freedom to start playing around with different weights of cord. Proper support, the strength of that support, and correct placement are how resonance (your true source of power and loudness) and a voice that sounds like one big register are achieved.

Hearing from the Outside

These ideas may be hard to grasp until you learn to change your acoustic perception to hear your voice as others do. You're going to want to push and squeeze your way through the break area, and you're going to think that the notes in that range won't sound strong unless you do.

Hearing from the outside as you practice, you're not going to like the way it sounds at first. It definitely won't feel or sound nearly as forceful. When using correct technique, you'll be thinking, "This can't be it. It feels and sounds like a head voice. It's way too wimpy." However, no matter what you're thinking while recording, you will be pleasantly surprised on playback. It will not sound like you expected. Instead, you will hear a stronger, brighter, bridged voice.

A Good Bridging Exercise: NEY

This is one of the exercises most favored by instructors to help bridge the passagio. The EH-EE diphthong keeps the throat open. N, like the other consonants we've used thus far, stops the flow of air by itself, so the exercise is performed without the tiny inhale following each note.

The N places the resonance a little more forward in the mask than other consonants because of where it is articulated. N is pronounced by placing the tip of the tongue on the front of the hard palate just behind the upper front teeth. The sides of the tongue touch the molars, creating a complete air seal. (As a side note, an L is pronounced the same way except air is allowed to escape around the sides of the tongue.) The tip of the tongue flips off the palate very quickly.

Training for Articulation

The mouth does not open and close with each NEY. Once your mouth reaches its open position, it **stays** in that position while you continue to pronounce NEYs. By maintaining this mouth formation, you train yourself to use only the tongue and palate to articulate the consonant. The jawbone is not one the articulators of consonants; it's only moving to facilitate production of the vowel. It only needs to do this a tiny bit on each NEY for this exercise.

We'll practice staccato and legato versions of this exercise, both starting with a single small inhalation. The octave roots (the 8s) for both versions may require that you leave out the EE and stay with EH to maintain an open throat in higher keys. Any modification other than this may close the throat. Remember to go back to the full EH-EE diphthong as soon as you can while still keeping the throat open.

CD PRACTICE TRACK 10 • 135 888 853 1 Men

CD PRACTICE TRACK 15 • 135 888 853 1 Women

CD DEMO TRACK 25 • 135 888 853 1 on NEYs

EXERCISE 12. 135 888 853 1 ON NEYS

Relax and then draw a small breath before each run. With each successively higher key, your upper abdominal region will require more diaphragmatic pressure (but not squeezing or tensing!) to expand for support. To keep the voice from breaking, slowly and evenly intensify the overall pressure as you make your way through the transition from the middle to high registers.

On the return from the higher registers through the passagio, keep the pressure even. If there is too much pressure on the way down, you will break. If there is not enough, you'll break. This is a place where a good instructor would help you find a balance, but if you don't have one, you're responsible for finding it yourself. If the diaphragm is unable to descend naturally to properly expand the upper abdominals, you'll also lose mask placement for resonance.

If you are having trouble maintaining support after several tries on the NEYs exercise, I suggest either trying it again with your hand below your navel to make sure your belly muscles aren't squeezing in and pushing up, or trying it again using the prop. If it's still not working, try going back to the other exercises using the prop for more practice, or taking a break from practice altogether.

CD PRACTICE TRACK 10 • 135 888 853 1 Men

CD PRACTICE TRACK 15 • 135 888 853 1 Women

CD DEMO TRACK 26 • 135 8—53 1 on NEY

EXERCISE 13. 135 8—53 1 ON NEY

The 135 8—53 1 legato NEY requires that you begin only the first note with an N, sustaining EH throughout the rest of the run, only merging into the EE vowel on the final note by slightly raising the sides of the tongue and bringing in the smile to raise the soft palate arches. Practicing this vocalise will help you gauge whether you are able to sustain equal loudness throughout a run. Listen closely to your tape for that steady stream of sound. Shaking, wobbling, or breaking will indicate you are holding the breath, or taking it in too heavily, or both.

XIV. Articulating a Difficult Consonant

For the next exercise, I've chosen the hard G because it is the consonant you'll feel stopping the flow of air more than any other, and the one singers have the most trouble with. Practice speaking the words "going good" aloud over and over, and you may feel and hear the cords close on the G. The problem with this consonant is in the reflexive urge to grab it forcefully and over-pronounce it with the vocal cords. Such massive glottal attack will create strain and interfere with resonance. We're going to move the focus of the G's pronunciation to the tongue, palate, and back teeth. You'll only emphasize the glottal attack if you want a dramatic effect.

Articulate the hard G from within the mouth, using the palate as a stop for the back of the tongue. Make this a quick action like the other consonants we've studied. In nearly every case, consonants should be performed with quick motions of the articulators so that the majority of tone is produced on vowels. This will make it easier to sing fluidly, especially as you ascend to higher registers in song.

This exercise connects the hard G to an OO that uses a continuous slide (called a *portamento*) from the 1 to the 5. Then you sing staccato GOOs from 4 down to 1 using the same breath.

 **CD PRACTICE TRACK 11** • 1-5 54321 Men

 **CD PRACTICE TRACK 16** • 1-5 54321 Women

 **CD DEMO TRACK 27** • Portamento Ascent to Descending GOOs 1-5 54321

EXERCISE 14. PORTAMENTO ASCENT TO DESCENDING GOOS 1-5 54321

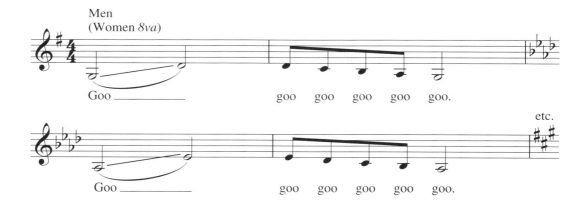

Use the hard G to propel the OO vowel into the mask and slide up from 1 to 5 with no breaks. Then start descending with separate GOOs from 5 down to 1. Every time you pronounce the G, you should feel the pressure of the tongue on the palate and upper back teeth, stopping the air for an almost imperceptible amount of time. Be careful not to grab that hard G with your cords. You can use a mirror to see the back of the tongue rise. As you progress through the keys, the change in range should be smooth all the way up and down, going from a thicker voice to a thinner one without breaking or switching from chest to head and back.

With this exercise, the lips will change their shape for OO. The properly-articulated G helps keep OO resonating. Listen to the tape to make sure you kept placement up at mouth level. If it sounds as if it dropped below the chin, it means you're losing the stretch of cord you need on this vowel, and the vowel has lost its shape.

OO is the airiest of all the vowels. The vocal cords *abduct* (move away from one another) the most on this vowel, though this is hard to see even with the laryngoscope. Because OO is so airy, many singers try to grab with their cords to give it more edge. Do not do this. If it feels and sounds airy to you, let it be. It is by keeping the OO resonating in the mask that you will work up to needed loudness. The strength and power for this vowel ultimately come from the diaphragmatic muscle regions, enabling you to add edge when you're ready.

Make sure your mouth does not open and then slightly close while performing this vocalise. The jaw must remain in place. Your lip shaping should remain consistent to keep the vowel sound OO resonating in the face. You can lightly place your fingers on either side of the jaw to make sure it does not move, even as you ascend in registers.

🔘 **CD PRACTICE TRACK 11** • 1-5 54321 Men

🔘 **CD PRACTICE TRACK 16** • 1-5 54321 Women

🔘 **CD DEMO TRACK 28** • Portamento 1-5, then Legato 54321 on GOO

EXERCISE 15. PORTAMENTO 1-5, THEN LEGATO 54321 ON GOO

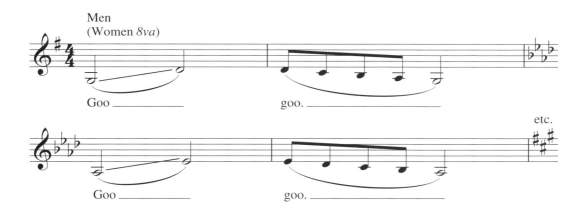

This vocalise starts the same as before, sliding from 1 to 5 on GOO. Without taking in a breath, pronounce another GOO on the same pitch and descend through 54321 on the OO only. As you switch from the OO to GOO on the top note (the 5), your jaw will move only very slightly for the articulation as you start the next GOO and descend to the last note with only the OO.

As with the previous exercises, feel free to try other consonant and vowel combinations on any single one of these exercises or others you've found that work for you outside of this book. In addition, you can use the prop any time you think you might need to build up more support of those diaphragmatic muscles, especially if you can feel and hear that you need more strength in any area.

XV. Phonetically Modifying Words in Song

Listen to CDs of different kinds of music and you will hear differences in pronunciation of the same words. One of the distinguishing characteristics of a musical genre is the way words are pronounced. Further, you will even hear differences between the ways two singers in the same genre approach the same song. Each has his or her own style. If you don't have your own style yet, pronunciation is one way to help you find it. Usually the singers who have sought me out find this part of our lessons very helpful and enlightening. They're also often surprised to find that a certain pronunciation is really a tool used to keep the throat open and create a specific placement.

We're going to do what many instructors call "working a song." Most concur this work is critical to achieving freedom for performance. Many will tell you to have a plan in place for every single song before you do a gig. If you planned and practiced, nothing takes you by surprise, you won't lose your placement, and you will feel free enough to emote, dance, and/or move all over the stage.

Before you start, you'll need a pen and paper. Choose a recorded song you like. First write out all the lyrics as they are spelled in English. Make sure to leave enough room to rewrite on the side, underneath, or over any line. By listening very carefully to how the singer pronounced his or her words, which may require extensive rewinding to make sure you caught it right, you will rewrite those words as they sounded phonetically when sung on the recording.

The way I have chosen to mark up my lyrics, mark where to breathe, and even mark how I want to perform a run is just a quick way that works best for me. Since you are doing this only for your own benefit, you can come up with your own way—something that makes sense and works for you. You'll need consistent phonetic spellings for all the consonants and vowel combinations in your songs, marks to show where breaths are needed, and marks to show exactly how you'd like to perform a run for style wherever you choose to place one. If you read music, just write your melodies and runs on the staff with the phonetically-spelled lyrics below and breath marks over the top. But don't let a lack of music notation skills stop you from doing this necessary work one way or another.

We'll look at examples in three different styles: country, pop, and rock, because they easily illustrate the principles we're learning with sounds that are easy to recognize and write out phonetically.

XV. Phonetically Modifying Words in Song

Country

💿 CD DEMO TRACK 29

Here is how I rewrote part of a line from a country song. Again, this is just my way; as long as you remember what you mean and are consistent about the way you represent specific sounds and techniques, you can do it any way you like. No one will be seeing this but you.

foot down on my accelerator

foot<u>d</u>ownuhn mah e<u>ks</u>elERadER/

Some words sound like they've run together to form only one, partly because of the drawl required for the country style. First, if I were to speak the words "foot down" aloud, I'd feel both the *t* and *d* pronounced using the tip of the tongue to touch the hard palate just behind the upper front teeth. Since they are both formed the same way, I will start with *t* but lean on the *d*, making the *t* barely perceptible. Because there is no breath between these two words, I've underlined the <u>td</u> to remind myself not to break up the two consonants and to sing the two words as one.

The *n* at the end of *down* is underlined because it also sounds like it's attached to the next word. The *n* at the end of *down* is used to propel the vowel sound in *on*, which should sound more like *uhn* than *ahn* for a slight country twang.

In country, *y* sounds as found in *my* are often drawn out, with the initial *ah* of the AH-EE diphthong given more emphasis than in other styles. In this case, the EE sound was left off entirely.

The *cc* in *accelerator* sounds like two different consonants. The first *c* is really a hard consonant that stops the flow of air, so I rewrite it as a *k* to avoid confusion about exactly what my articulators will be doing. The second *c* sounds like an *s*. The *k* and *s* sounds run together, so I underline them to remind myself that they are connected. The *k* is pronounced at the back of the raised tongue by lightly touching the palate. I go straight from the click of *k* the to an *s* formed by channeling the tongue near the palate, using it to propel the *eh* vowel that follows into the mask and out of the mouth.

Within this same word are two Rs. Each must be exaggerated for the country sound. By writing ER in capitals, I know to stress both Rs. Lastly there is a *t* in the spelling of *accelerator*. That *t* sounds like a *d* to me when sung country style, hence the *d* in the phoneticized version. At this point, a new phrase is about to begin, so I have added a slash mark to remind myself to take in a tiny breath before I start it.

Practicing the Phonetics

Once you have the lyrics written out phonetically, I suggest completely crossing out the originals and only looking at the newly rewritten ones as you start to practice singing the song. It's okay to work on a little piece at a time until you have the entire song memorized exactly the way it is pronounced on the original version. When working on fragments like this, don't start from the beginning of the song every time. Just go to the next spot that needs work. Then go back and start stringing bigger pieces together.

When you're ready, start singing the entire song along with the recording, keeping your pencil ready to mark spots that give you trouble so you can come back and practice them in isolation. If it takes looking at, reading, and singing your phonetically-spelled lyrics fifty times over until it's memorized, then that is what you'll have to do.

After I got really good at the markup process, I no longer needed to write out every single consonant and vowel as they sounded versus the way they were spelled. After applying it to several songs, the process becomes more automatic. When I work a song today, I only have to mark where the consonants aren't true to themselves, when three words might sound like one, if they sound much different from how they're normally spoken, and I mark the runs so I know where I'm going with them.

> If you are interested in learning more about phonetics, a library is a good place to start your research. Books on phonetics create standard sets of rules for symbols, to spell out words exactly as they sound when spoken. There is an international phonetic alphabet for all languages that may be of special interest to non-native English speakers or those with accents they wish to modify.

Some styles often have the ends of words losing pronunciation of a consonant. I might cross through those letters with a slash mark. Words that are sung with less edge and consonant articulation like this often happen in R&B.

When you start singing the way it's sounded out, you may discover that you need even *more* support from the diaphragmatic muscle group regions, especially as you try to sing through more difficult sections of any song. If this is the case, you might want to go back to using the prop while singing just to remind yourself of that needed additional strength and power.

Pop

💿 CD DEMO TRACK 30

Now here's a phonetic interpretation of a line from a pop song. The first thing you'll notice is that the letter R doesn't get the emphasis it does in country.

You better not start, no

Yoo behduh nah(t)stah(rt)/noh/

You bet - ter   not   start,   no. _____

On *you,* the vowel sound is OO. For this style (and this song in particular), the last letters of some words are pronounced very lightly, or not at all. With the word *better,* the *r* is not pronounced, so I dropped it altogether. The first vowel is a short *e* (as in the word *led*) rather than a long one (as in the word *feet*), so I changed the spelling to EH.

Again we are faced with a double consonant, *tt.* When sung with an American English accent, it's pronounced as only one consonant, a *d,* which should be used to propel the following UH into the mask. The last *r* in *better* was not sung, so the word ends with the UH vowel sound.

For the word *not,* the O sounds like an AH. The *t* is a little tricky here. It is formed by placing the tip of the tongue on the hard palate just behind the upper front teeth without finishing its entire pronunciation, creating a silent stop. For style, I want to create what sounds like a break between the two words *not start*, but without taking a breath in between. Once the tip of the tongue is on the hard palate, I will use the pressure from it to stress the *st* of the next word. This pressurized *t* going to the *st* propels the vowel AH. Next I added parentheses at (*rt*) to remind myself that the end of this word is barely pronounced for this style.

A distinct break is created between the two words *start* and *no* without a breath, but I marked it with a slash to make sure the *n* stops the flow of air for that break. Finally, I wrote the O as OH to make sure I shape a long O as in the word *go*. At the end of that word, and just before the next phrase starts, I have to take another short breath, so I placed a slash mark after the *no*.

Musical Shorthand

For a melodic run on a single syllable (a *melisma*), I add an arrow following its general contour over that word. If the run includes many notes, I'll find those notes on the keyboard and write them down alongside the arrow. This way I'll know exactly which notes I'm singing for that run. Should there be a note that sustains a long time, I place a horizontal arrow above the word and extend it across the top to remind myself that this is where I want to really prolong this note. If there is vibrato, I might make a squiggly line above or at the end of a word.

In the previous example, the word *no* is sung with a run, using a few descending notes that move from one to the other swiftly. To make a note of this, I will draw a downward arrow over that word and write in what each one of those notes really is so I will know exactly where I'm going without losing pitch. If the melodic direction were to change from down to up (or vice versa), I'd add a zigzag to my arrow.

Rock Placement

This style can be difficult to learn. Often, to the listener, it sounds like shouting—and sometimes it is, depending on the effect desired. However, for the most part rock is **talk**, not yelling all the way through a song. Should you choose to yell, my best advice is to seek out teachers who specialize in these types of effects so you can learn how to do it without trashing your vocal cords.

The placement for rock is more vertical than that of the previous two styles. The vertical direction of air and sound helps keep the throat more open for that fuller sound. At the same time, the sound absolutely must resonate fully in the mask. This is one of the main things any rock singer must learn if he or she wants lasting power without damage.

The style can also require more diaphragmatic support than usual to give strength and power to different sections of a song, but it must not overpower the vocal cords. The pronunciation of the words should be about the same as they are when spoken, though the consonants should still be executed by quick motions of the articulators alone to propel the vowel sounds as in all other styles. Rock singers who use the throat or breathing muscles for consonants can lose their voices quickly.

Rock

 **CD DEMO TRACK 31**

giving a high five

gihvihnuh/hah<u>y</u> fah<u>y</u>(v)

In the phonetically-spelled rock example, it sounds to me like the hard G propels an IH vowel (as in the word *hit*); the same happens on VIH. The second G isn't pronounced at all. Instead, the N in *gihvihn* propels us right into the next vowel, *a*, which actually sounds like an UH. Because the N goes straight into the *a*, it sounds like one word instead of two, so I have written it out that way: *gihvihnuh*.

There is a very, very quick breath after the words *giving a*, and before the word *high*. The slash mark reminds me to take one in. Also, this word sounds like HA-EE to me. I underlined the y because it is a diphthong and leans more towards that EE vowel. There is no breath between *high* and *five*, but these words are pronounced separately. So I left a space between them, but no slash mark. With the word *fahyv*, the pronunciation also seems to lean toward the EE of the AH-EE diphthong, so I underlined that y. Since the *v* of this word is barely pronounced, I added parentheses around it.

The Wrong Form of Emulation

If you should sing along with your favorite CD for a bit, do not make it as loud or as forceful as you are hearing that singer on CD. If you think about it, in reality, do you know of anyone who actually has a large condenser microphone, preamp, compressor, and reverb technology attached inside their neck and vocal cords? Do not yell, even if it sounds as if you have to in order to get the kind of power and loudness you think you're hearing.

Tape yourself shouting and yelling as much as you think you have to for any style, and notice how hard it gets the higher you have to sing in the song. You may even feel you are choking on the words. Shouting and yelling forces you to blow the sound out from having taken in too much air. The cords will not be able to control the flow of air as you sing.

Now play back what you just yelled out/sang, and you'll hear what I mean for yourself. Most likely, it won't sound the way you thought it did from inside your head, and you probably won't like it at all. You may even find yourself getting frustrated because of how uncomfortable it feels and how distorted it sounds. After repeatedly going after it the same wrong way, you may even begin to think and feel that you will never able to sing these things well or right, and never like **that** singer does.

Combine this incorrect perception of how to achieve a powerful tone with the need to overcome the loudness of a band and you'll end up really hurting your voice over time.

If you sing with a band, get your own microphone and your own monitor at the very least. Don't rely on what others may or may not have for you. Take the time to find the mic that works best with your voice and singing style.

In-ear monitoring systems are the best, but they're also expensive. If these are beyond your budget, there are still plenty of good monitors that will do the job. Do the research to find which will work best for you and your wallet. If you're serious about singing in clubs, you're best off having at least part ownership of the PA system your band uses, so that you have some control over it.

If you can hear yourself well through a monitor and don't feel or hear strain, chances are your audience can hear you just as well, and you'll sound good to them. If you can't hear yourself, you'll risk misusing your instrument to the point of damage. Change the monitor mix, point the guitar amps away from you, and/or isolate the drum set with a baffle. Band members may have to play more quietly. If their equipment blows up from abuse, they can go out and replace it. You can't do this with your voice.

The Right Form of Emulation

If you know what to listen for on the CDs you hear and spend a lot of time recording and listening to your own voice, you'll notice that your favorite singers probably aren't screaming and yelling as much as you thought. The sound you're after comes from inhaling the correct amount of air, not holding your breath, keeping tones at mouth level, keeping mask resonance, maintaining a practiced balance of diaphragmatic support and cord engagement, and correct articulation: all the things we've been practicing in this book.

Trying to convey a rock attitude by squeezing, pushing, or overblowing the cords doesn't work, and it is not what you are hearing. Pay close attention to the pronunciation of each consonant and vowel combination you hear, analyze it, write it down, and then sing what you have written. Articulation of the consonants is especially critical to keeping placement, support, strength, and resonance. Should you choose to pronounce some words differently, it should be for style of song and effect and not something repeatedly executed in every song because you don't know any other way.

XVI. Scalifying Difficult Words and Song Sections

Here we sing through scale exercises, using a deliberately-chosen line of lyrics from a song instead of repeated consonants and vowels as in earlier sections. It's obviously going to be a bit harder, so please be patient.

Often when we are singing, we encounter sections of songs that require us to go from a relatively easy note to a higher, more difficult one in an instant, and vice versa, even as we pronounce challenging words and phrases. There are also many songs that would sound best if we were to stay with a one-register sound on upper-middle to high notes all the way through an entire section. At this point, we aren't just faced with getting hung up on consonants, but also the melodies.

When dealing with these obstacles at this point in your development, dropping off in sound, lowering your larynx, or releasing support should be rapidly turning into non-options. Instead, we'll face the problems head on by exercising the use of the articulators on the problem spots in isolation, by taking sections with those particular words and bringing them to vocalises.

When I first began concocting this solution, I tried many different exercises with difficult sections in songs to sing. After trying many out, I found that I preferred using major scale degrees 1234 54321 or just 54321, depending on which direction—up or down—I had to go in the song. You probably won't need any more complicated note sequences than these. Once you can execute them throughout your range with the correct articulation, you'll be ready to go back and tackle the lyric using the original melody of the song.

💿 CD DEMO TRACK 32

Burn - ing   me   up _____   in - side. _____

This is an excerpt from a song that was giving me trouble on the notes leading to the word *up*, ascending from A♯ to C♯, exactly the place in my upper-middle register where I'd tend to break if I pushed. My preference turned out to be the vocalise 1234 54321 because it ascends as well as descends—similar to what occurs in the song. The excerpt is set to the vocalise and spelled phonetically below for you to practice through your range.

💿 CD PRACTICE TRACK 8 • 1234 54321 Men

💿 CD PRACTICE TRACK 13 • 1234 54321 Women

💿 CD DEMO TRACK 33 • Scalifying Lyric with 1234 54321

EXERCISE 16. SCALIFYING LYRIC WITH 1234 54321

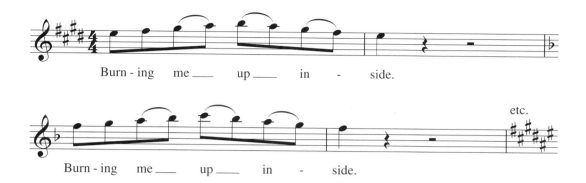

bur ni(ng) me- ee uh- uh pih- ihn sah(y)d

The word *up* is the highest note of the original phrase and at my break area in song. I wanted to make sure I placed that particular word on the top note of the scale, so I intentionally spread the previous three syllables (*bur ning me*) over the first four notes by extending the word *me*. I also wanted to keep the word *up* as two syllables the way it was in the song, so its vowel sound UH extends through 5 and 4 of the descending scale. Next, on the way down, scale degree 3 starts with the P popping off the lips as in the word *pin*. Extend the IH sound through scale step 2, and emphasize the AH of the AH-EE diphthong on the last note. Let the vowel sustain for the full value of the quarter note, just tacking the *d* on at the end.

Working the New Vocalise

From G above middle C (G4 in scientific pitch notation) to C5 is my break area. I prefer working vocalises like these through two octaves of my range to extend past the break area on both sides. Usually, I'll choose G3 (G below middle C) to begin and ascend chromatically key by key until I've reached G5 with the top note of the vocalise. Once I've reached a run where the top note is G5 (in this case, the run that starts on C5), I will start my descent key by key until I've come back down to G3 as the root.

If there are some trouble spots on the way up or on the way back down in any key, I will stop and work that area separately using the same exercise (1234 54321) until it's right. The demo track begins just below my break area; I would continue to repeat this section until I get it right. Getting it right requires focusing on articulating the consonants so they can propel the vowel sounds easily and without strain.

Your break area is probably different from mine. It's something every singer, even beginners, should make sure to know: which pitches on the keyboard are in your break range? Practice the vocalise starting well below this range, continue until you are completely past it, and then start lowering the keys again, until you end up where you started.

Wasn't that fun? Let's try another. Here's a phrase where I had a problem with keeping the lowest note at mouth level.

💿 CD DEMO TRACK 34

Musically speaking, it's a descending A minor triad arpeggio in the song, but for the exercise, we'll uniformly apply a descending major scale from 5 to 1 to any descending phrase. You could work the original phrase from your song—whatever it is—through your range, but you'd have to be able to play it in every key, which can be a lot of extra work if you're not an accomplished pianist. This way you can focus on your articulation and placement, and of course you'll still be hitting every note in the range, using the same words.

💿 CD PRACTICE TRACK 7 • 54321 Men

💿 CD PRACTICE TRACK 12 • 54321 Women

💿 CD DEMO TRACK 35 • Scalifying High-to-Low Lyric with 54321

EXERCISE 17. SCALIFYING HIGH-TO-LOW LYRIC WITH 54321

yootooklee-erlee

The first three syllables of the phrase each get their own pitch. The word "clear" is spread over scale degrees 3 and 2, so that the phrase ends with the syllable "ly" on the tonic note of the scale on a strong beat. Try to arrange your lyrics across the scale in a musically sensible way.

I want to hit the final A3 of the original phrase in my low register with dead-on pitch and edge, so I made sure the lowest note of the first run, G3, is well below the pitch I have to hit in the song. The more stretch I can get in the lowest and highest of my registers in the exercise, the better chance I'll have of hitting notes easily in song that are not quite as low or high.

I ascend with this exercise from key to key until I reach G5 as the top note at the beginning of this vocalise, meaning the highest run will be in the key of C. Then I again descend until I reach the point I started from, ending the final run on G3.

Just as with the previous exercise, you have to determine for yourself where you should start and how high you should go. If you run into any trouble spots on ascent or descent, stop right there and work those notes separately. Having to stick with one run until it's right will help the other registers because you are trying to learn new habitual actions of the articulators.

Here's the last time I'll hit you over the head. If you can't hear whether any notes slipped off pitch with your own ears as you execute the exercise, you must go to the tape and listen. If any pitch dropped down in the slightest, it means you did not use enough articulation effort. If you get lazy and decide not to repractice to get it right, then you will be inviting incorrect habits to come back.

Sometimes an instructor will ask you to lower or raise your larynx when vocalizing. This instruction may be given to help guide you into proper placement. If your placement is already established, the same instruction could apply to creating an effect in the pursuit of your own style.

The instructor may also warn you not to keep practicing this same way because it could create an incorrect habit. When singing with artistic expression in song, informed choices allow you to sound just about any way you want. However, informed choices can only be made once you've acquired a good vocal foundation for performing styles without causing injury to the mechanism.

Warming Up for a Gig

Recognizing the condition of your vocal mechanism before a show is critical to your success. If you are tired, or if your cords have swelling or mucus, it will be especially necessary to warm up with exercises you already know before singing songs at your usual volume. The exercises in this book aren't just about increasing the strength, power, and endurance of the voice; they are also designed to be used for warming up before singing a gig. During your warm-up, an exercise may reveal where the voice is weak and where you might find yourself running into trouble.

When you get to an area that's weaker than the rest, then make an informed decision about which other exercise(s) might help that area most. Go to work on that area alone until it opens up. After that, test out your entire range by going through the exercise once. Observe, listen, and physically sense whether you were successful at working out those kinks. If during the course of your test run you find another area that may need some work, do the same thing and test again.

On all of these exercises, every note should be of equal loudness. No pitch should be louder than the previous one, especially as you go higher. That would mean you are pushing, and your voice will break at some point. Start over with a level of loudness that doesn't feel like your usual force, even if it sounds like a head voice to you.

By now, you should be able to determine which exercise will remind the voice of right action and open up the throat in the trouble spots. This will boost your confidence and enable you to perform your magic on stage without worry.

Conclusion

Most instructors teach whatever they learned that worked for them as singers. Go to any bookstore and read through books on breath technique for singers and you will find many different ways of going about it. I've tried a lot of them, but things didn't change for me until I discovered that breath control has just as much to do with the art of singing as the cords do. It became clear that, if the air is *taken in correctly*, the necessary diaphragmatic support will be there, the cords will engage, and the cords will control the flow of air as you exhale sounds.

For all of you who have found your way to this book, I hope I've helped you put some of the puzzle pieces together.

Appendix: Breathing Techniques for Meditation Versus Singing

Meditative breathing is highly recommended by instructors for singers but usually only as a way to release any built-up tension in the mind and body. However, it doesn't work for everyone. Many prefer stretching exercises for the face, neck, and body. It's a personal choice.

Over the years, I've frequently been asked about applying the breathing techniques used in yoga or meditation for singing, and I recommend against it. Because so many singers have thought they could use those techniques, I decided to do a little investigating on my own.

What Didn't Work for Singing

I ordered ten different CDs that focused on using the breath for meditation. I also read a book that offered over a hundred different techniques. After practicing with all the CDs and many of the exercises in the book, I came to the conclusion that most could not be used for singing. It was not a waste of time, because I do meditate daily, but I found only two methods that complemented the breath technique I teach.

First, let me briefly talk about some popular meditative breathing techniques that I **don't** recommend for use while singing.

1. Breathe through the nose, not the mouth.

The advantages of this are that, as air enters the nose, it is warmed up and humidified by its mucus lining, the hair follicles filter out dust particles, and enzymes in the mucus clean out bacteria. The air that then reaches the lungs is warm and of good quality. When exhaling, the warm moist air from the lungs humidifies the nasal cavity.

The disadvantages with it come when inhaling to sing. I found that the nasal passageway tended to collapse and close as I tried to suck in enough air. This forced me to hold my breath for a moment before I started to sing. It's much easier to take air in quickly and in quantity by using the mouth. (Air may very well be coming through my nose at the same time, but I don't feel it.)

If you have been taught to breath through the nose and you don't have a problem holding the breath or any kind of discomfort that could potentially lead to abuse or damage, it's okay to stick with it.

2. Inhale, pause lightly, then release.

As discussed and demonstrated throughout this book, holding the breath will create the need to tense the lower belly muscles to keep the air from escaping too fast. After that, those muscles will have to squeeze and push up the air to force the sound out. You will lose your diaphragmatic support, and over time, create damage.

3. Alternate between movement and stillness.

To *alternate* means to do one thing, then switch to another, and then switch back again. *Stillness* just means "not moving." This instruction requires that you take in the air and switch to holding it before switching back to movement i.e., exhaling. Again, this means holding your breath, which is bad for singing.

4. Prolong the inhalation by taking it in through the nose, hold it in, and then exhale at a measured pace or for a specified count.

This is a common meditative instruction and couldn't be clearer, but most of it is wrong for singing. The only part I can agree with is the control of exhalation when phonating.

What Did Work

Bearing in mind that I was unable to try every technique available, I only found two in my samples that support the breathing technique I teach singers.

1. Simply allow air to come out naturally before taking in a new breath, like a cycle with no beginning or end.

The author of this book stated that most people studying meditation don't care for this technique, because it doesn't do as much for them as intentional deep breathing does. Yet it is a method that reinforces the premise that taking in the breath and singing are like one action.

2. Do not force the breath in any way, and avoid straining by sucking in the abdomen.

I agree.

Glossary of Voice-Related Instructional Terms
WEBSTER'S NEW WORLD DICTIONARY, THIRD COLLEGE EDITION, MACMILLAN, 1994.

abdomen	the part of the body between the rib cage and the pelvic girdle
abduct	to pull away from the median axis, as in vocal cords moving apart
acoustic	sound as heard by others
adduct	pulling toward the median axis, as in vocal cords coming together
airy	containing air in its movement
amplitude	the measurement of the extremes of a vibration
anteriorly	toward the front
articulate	to speak distinctly
attention	the keeping of one's mind on one thing only, exclusive of anything else
aware	conscious of one or two things at the same time; inclusive of other things
bear	to support and carry the weight
belt	to sing loudly and lustily with a driving rhythm, usually without force
billow	large swelling or surge of sound
blast	increased air pressure caused by an abrupt application of force
blow	to force out air by blasting
bracing tension	strength and solidity for supporting weight
break	to collapse or come apart
breath	a voiceless inhalation or exhalation of air
breathy	sound containing more than the normal amount of exhaled air
bridge	to connect one register to another
burst	explode
cartilage	a tough almost bony yet elastic-like tissue
close	with little or no space between
compress	to reduce the space occupied by a given amount
constrict	to narrow by squeezing

contemplate	to think about intently
contiguous	switching from in to out with no break in between
continual	happening repeatedly
continuous	going on without interruption
contract	to compress by pulling into a more compact form
converge	to come together, meet
depth	intensity; deeper part in singing
diaphragm	large dome-shaped muscles and tendons that separate the chest cavity from the abdominal cavity
diphthong	a sound formed by two merged vowels that have two target positions; the first vowel sound starts in one position, and the second vowel sound ends in another
distort	to twist out of shape
draw	to take air into the mouth
edge	sharp, keen, bright, focused intensity
efficiency	producing desired effects with the least amount of effort
effort	energetic exertion of mental and/or physical power
enunciate	to pronounce words clearly and distinctly
epiglottis	thin lidlike cartilage attached to the back of the tongue that folds over the opening of the windpipe during swallowing to prevent food or liquid from passing through the vocal cords and entering the lungs
exert	to put forth energetically
exhale	to breathe out
expand	to spread out
expel	to drive out by force
false cords or folds	also called ventricular folds, the pair of thick mucous membranes that protect and sit slightly superior to the more delicate true vocal cords or folds; they have a minimal role in normal phonation but are often used in musical screaming and the death grunt singing style; also used in Tuvan throat singing.
feel	to perceive through physical sensation
firm	not moved or shaken easily under pressure; fixed and stable
fluid	flow and movement that does not separate under pressure
focus	to pay attention to one thing only

force	to exert beyond one's natural capacity; strain
girth	part of body between ribs and hips
glide	to flow smoothly or easily
glottis	space between the vocal cords
grit/rasp	a rough grating added to clean sound for stylistic effect
hard consonant	a sound that stops the flow of air when speaking or singing
heavy	with great weight, force, or impact
hesitate	pause or stop momentarily
hold	to grip or grasp to keep from breaking free
hum	to sing with the lips closed and without producing words
imperceptible	so slight it can't be distinguished easily
impulse	sudden inclination to act without thinking first
ingrained	firmly established
inhale	to draw air into the lungs
inherent	part of its natural constitution; innate
instinct	an unlearned response
intuition	immediate understanding (either known or learned) used without conscious thought
jump	a bouncing action
knowledge	understanding gained after one has learned from the experience
larynx	the structure of muscle and cartilage at the upper end of the human trachea, containing the vocal cords and serving as the organ of the voice
laryngologist	medical doctor who specializes in diseases of the larynx and its adjacent parts
laryngoscopy	an examination of the larynx by means of a laryngoscope
legato	smoothly-connected notes with no break in between
let go	to offer no resistance; allow
lick	swiftly moving notes inserted over an existing composition, whether improvisational or planned
light	without your usual force
listen	to make a conscious effort to hear
loud	great intensity of sound

median	a line joining midpoints
morph	change back to its specified form
navel	centrally located abdominal depression; belly button
octave	the distance between two pitches that have the same letter name, eight steps apart in the major scale
open	free for passage
pant	to breathe rapidly
passagio	(Italian) the passage of pitches that need to be connected for a one-register sound
pause	temporary stop, short period of inaction, hesitation
perception	ability to grasp a concept through senses, awareness
pharyngeal	in the region of the pharynx
pharynx	the muscular and membranous cavity of the alimentary canal leading from the mouth and nasal passages to the larynx and esophagus
phonetics	the study of spoken or sung sounds and their representation by written symbols
pop off	create with a short, light, sudden, and very quick motion of the lips
portamento	a continuous gliding from one note to another
pressure	a condition of emphasis to maintain steady weight
principles	fundamentals of technique
process	continuing development involving many steps and changes
pronounce	to articulate a sound, word, or syllable
propel	to move forward without pushing or using the force of the breath
puff	quick drawing in of breath
pump	to drive air into
push	exert pressure against; thrust up
reflex	automatic response
release	the method of ending a tone by liberating the air without blowing
resistance	an opposition of forces that hinders movement
root	1. origin, cause; 2. the tonic note of scale, chord, or key
run	series of notes, as in a vocalise or lick
sense	generalized feeling; awareness

sensation	the power of receiving conscious impressions through the body
shove	to push roughly
shut	to close an opening
simultaneous	occurring at the same time
siren	a prolonged sound that steadily descends, ascends, or both
smooth	with even consistency, flowing
softness	absence of harsh intensity
soft consonant	a sound that only partially blocks the flow of air
solid	firm, strong
speech pathology	a branch of medicine dealing with injury caused by abnormalities or variations in vocal sound production
spurt	to expel, as in a short stream of air
squeeze	to force together by pressing tightly
staccato	with distinct breaks through successive tones
steady	constant; unwavering; maintaining a state of equilibrium
strain	to force beyond normal limits
stream	a continuously flowing supply
strength	the power to resist strain and stress
suck	to take in so much air that your body compresses and contracts
support	bearing the weight of the column of air to keep the cords from collapsing
surge	any strong increase of energy
sustain	to maintain or prolong
taut	firm but not tight or strained
tense	tight or strained
thick	more depth
thin	without depth
throat	the upper part of the passage that leads from the nose and mouth down into the pharynx, larynx, and trachea
thrust	sudden gush of air

tight	so packed together that no air can pass through
ventricular folds	also known as the false cords; membranous structures that protect the more delicate true cords responsible for sound and pitch
vestibular folds	see *ventricular folds*
vocal cords or folds	elastic-like structures in the larynx responsible for phonation
vocalise	a singing exercise
vocalis muscle	the middle of the vocal cord
vocal ligament	the inner edge of the vocal cord
vocalize	to sing or speak
volume	loudness
waist	part of body between ribs and hips; same as girth
wavering	unsteady
weak	lacking strength; unable to resist strain or pressure

About the Author

DENA MURRAY
WWW.DENAMURRAY.COM

Dena Murray was born in Los Angeles, CA, where she began her singing career at the age of 12. Her performance career included musical theatre productions, television and motion picture work, and singing for radio commercials. Specializing in vocal technique instruction for over 20 years, her passion has been to help singers achieve their dreams.

In 1994, Dena joined the teaching staff at the Musicians Institute in Hollywood, CA. From 1996–2006, she coordinated the technique taught by all instructors and wrote the curriculum for the vocal department.

Since leaving MI, Dena teaches privately in home and online, working with both beginning and professional singers world-wide. Some of her former students include Holly Valentine (Hyper Crush), Sarah Hudson (Ultraviolet Sound), John Hensley ("As the World Turns," CBS) Christina & Michael Salerno (Within the Eddy), Lauren Adams, demo-and-session artists, along with talent from CBS, NBC, HBO, motion picture films, and television. She is also a key Subject Matter Expert for TheModernVocalist.com (a large and growing website serving the needs of vocalists all over the world), and Patron for VIDLA (Vocalist International Distance Learning Academy).

Dena's first book, *Vocal Technique: A Guide to Finding Your Real Voice* (Hal Leonard Publications, 2002), features an introduction to the vocal mechanism and how it works, why it can be necessary to separate the head and chest registers before bridging for one-register sound, and exactly how to develop the voice.

Her second book, co-authored by Tita Hutchison, *Advanced Vocal Technique: Middle Voice, Placement, and Styles* (Hal Leonard Publications, 2008) is a combination of both authors' experiences, teaching a unique method for proper mask placement through physical sensations and how to practically apply the method to all styles of singing.

Vocal Strength & Power: Boost Your Singing with Proper Technique and Breathing (Hal Leonard Publications, 2009) contains little-known secrets behind the art of breath technique, how to achieve true loudness, strength, endurance, and increase of range for a much more powerful one-register sound and singing voice.

Dena graduated from Ithaca College, Ithaca, NY, with a Bachelor of Science in Speech.

Dedication

To Carlos Barrios, Terapat Chearapong, Pontus Duvjso, Peter Hogberg, and Michael Salerno. These five singers have believed so much in my talent as a master technique teacher and coach that they allowed me to use them to prove my theory. I cannot thank these men enough for their burning desire to gain control over their voices, each with their own gifted talents, and their hearts.

My deepest gratitude also goes to:

BT, for having been one of the greatest gifts in my life. I could not have written this book without you standing right behind me every step of the way all these years. Piece of my heart.

Kurt Plahna, Hal Leonard Corp. for all your support and inspirational ideas.

Jeff Schroedl, Hal Leonard Corp. for your high regard, confidence, and belief in me as an author. I am truly appreciative.

My family: my son, Jason; my mother, Iris; my brother, Andy; and my sister, Bonnie—for being there for me, giving me all the support you possibly could during these last few months, and for putting up with the unplugging of my phone and cell for so many weeks, yet always coming up with ways to connect with me in spite of it. You mean the world to me.

My dear, tragically departed father—our **Johnny-one-note**, famous among all those who knew him for reading one book a day, who'd have been so proud knowing his daughter wrote books, would've studied from each, practiced, and **endlessly** asked, "Is this right?"

Ann Howley and Janet Rickey, for their long-standing friendship, trust, loyalty, and faith in me as a person and in my work.

Mike Campbell, the man responsible for the launch of my career so many years ago. There was never anyone in my life that believed in me more than he did when we began working together. He brought me on board as an instructor at the Musicians Institute VIT program in 1994, trusted me with the privilege of heading up the vocal technique program from 1996–2006, gave me the opportunity to write the curriculum for that program and to share my unique method of teaching technique to the students of VIT. He will forever have a very special place in my heart.

Most of all, my loving HP.

Pro Vocal® Series
SONGBOOK & SOUND-ALIKE CD
*SING 8 GREAT SONGS
WITH A PROFESSIONAL BAND*

Whether you're a karaoke singer or a auditioning professional, the Pro Vocal® series is for you! Unlike most karaoke packs, each book in the Pro Vocal Series contains the lyric melody, and chord symbols for eight hit song. The CD contains demos for listening, an separate backing tracks so you can sing alon. The CD is playable on any CD player, but it is als enhanced so PC and Mac computer users ca adjust the recording to any pitch without changir the tempo! Perfect for home rehearsal, partie auditions, corporate events, and gigs without backup band.

WOMEN'S EDITIONS

00740246	**1. Broadway Songs**	$14.95
00740249	**2. Jazz Standards**	$14.95
00740246	**3. Contemporary Hits**	$14.95
00740277	**4. '80s Gold**	$12.95
00740299	**5. Christmas Standards**	$15.95
00740281	**6. Disco Fever**	$12.95
00740279	**7. R&B Super Hits**	$12.95
00740309	**8. Wedding Gems**	$12.95
00740409	**9. Broadway Standards**	$14.95
00740348	**10. Andrew Lloyd Webber**	$14.95
00740344	**11. Disney's Best**	$14.99
00740378	**12. Ella Fitzgerald**	$14.95
00740350	**14. Musicals of Boublil & Schönberg**	$14.95
00740377	**15. Kelly Clarkson**	$14.95
00740342	**16. Disney Favorites**	$14.95
00740353	**17. Jazz Ballads**	$14.99
00740376	**18. Jazz Vocal Standards**	$14.95
00740375	**20. Hannah Montana**	$16.95
00740354	**21. Jazz Favorites**	$14.99
00740374	**22. Patsy Cline**	$14.95
00740369	**23. Grease**	$14.95
00740367	**25. ABBA**	$14.95
00740365	**26. Movie Songs**	$14.95
00740360	**28. High School Musical 1 & 2**	$14.95
00740363	**29. Torch Songs**	$14.95
00740379	**30. Hairspray**	$14.95
00740380	**31. Top Hits**	$14.95
00740384	**32. Hits of the '70s**	$14.95
00740388	**33. Billie Holiday**	$14.95
00740389	**34. The Sound of Music**	$15.99
00740390	**35. Contemporary Christian**	$14.95
00740392	**36. Wicked**	$15.99
00740393	**37. More Hannah Montana**	$14.95
00740394	**38. Miley Cyrus**	$14.95
00740396	**39. Christmas Hits**	$15.95
00740410	**40. Broadway Classics**	$14.95
00740415	**41. Broadway Favorites**	$14.99
00740416	**42. Great Standards You Can Sing**	$14.99
00740417	**43. Singable Standards**	$14.99
00740418	**44. Favorite Standards**	$14.99
00740419	**45. Sing Broadway**	$14.99
00740420	**46. More Standards**	$14.99
00740421	**47. Timeless Hits**	$14.95
00740422	**48. Easygoing R&B**	$14.99
00740424	**49. Taylor Swift**	$14.99
00740425	**50. From This Moment On**	$14.99
00740430	**52. Worship Favorites**	$14.99

MEN'S EDITIONS

00740248	**1. Broadway Songs**	$14.95
00740250	**2. Jazz Standards**	$14.95
00740251	**3. Contemporary Hits**	$14.99
00740278	**4. '80s Gold**	$12.95
00740298	**5. Christmas Standards**	$15.95
00740280	**6. R&B Super Hits**	$12.95
00740282	**7. Disco Fever**	$12.95
00740310	**8. Wedding Gems**	$12.95
00740411	**9. Broadway Greats**	$14.99
00740333	**10. Elvis Presley – Volume 1**	$14.95
00740349	**11. Andrew Lloyd Webber**	$14.95
00740345	**12. Disney's Best**	$14.95
00740347	**13. Frank Sinatra Classics**	$14.95
00740334	**14. Lennon & McCartney**	$14.99
00740335	**16. Elvis Presley – Volume 2**	$14.99
00740343	**17. Disney Favorites**	$14.95
00740351	**18. Musicals of Boublil & Schönberg**	$14.95
00740346	**20. Frank Sinatra Standards**	$14.95
00740341	**24. Duke Ellington**	$14.99
00740359	**26. Pop Standards**	$14.99
00740362	**27. Michael Bublé**	$14.95
00740361	**28. High School Musical 1 & 2**	$14.95
00740364	**29. Torch Songs**	$14.95
00740366	**30. Movie Songs**	$14.95
00740368	**31. Hip Hop Hits**	$14.95
00740370	**32. Grease**	$14.95
00740371	**33. Josh Groban**	$14.95
00740373	**34. Billy Joel**	$17.99
00740381	**35. Hits of the '50s**	$14.95
00740382	**36. Hits of the '60s**	$14.95
00740383	**37. Hits of the '70s**	$14.95
00740385	**38. Motown**	$14.95
00740386	**39. Hank Williams**	$14.95
00740387	**40. Neil Diamond**	$14.99
00740391	**41. Contemporary Christian**	$14.95
00740397	**42. Christmas Hits**	$15.95
00740399	**43. Ray**	$14.95
00740400	**44. The Rat Pack Hits**	$14.99
00740401	**45. Songs in the Style of Nat "King" Cole**	$14.99
00740402	**46. At the Lounge**	$14.95
00740403	**47. The Big Band Singer**	$14.95
00740404	**48. Jazz Cabaret Songs**	$14.99
00740405	**49. Cabaret Songs**	$14.99
00740406	**50. Big Band Standards**	$14.99
00740412	**51. Broadway's Best**	$14.99
00740427	**52. Great Standards Collection**	$19.99
00740431	**53. Worship Favorites**	$14.99

MIXED EDITIONS
These editions feature songs for both mal and female voices.

00740311	**1. Wedding Duets**	$12.9
00740398	**2. Enchanted**	$14.9
00740407	**3. Rent**	$14.9
00740408	**4. Broadway Favorites**	$14.9
00740413	**5. South Pacific**	$15.9
00740414	**6. High School Musical 3**	$14.9
00740429	**7. Christmas Carols**	$14.9

FOR MORE INFORMATION, SEE YOUR LOCAL MUSIC DEALER, OR WRITE TO:

HAL•LEONARD®
CORPORATION
7777 W. BLUEMOUND RD. P.O. BOX 13819 MILWAUKEE, WI 53213

Visit Hal Leonard online at www.halleonard.c

Prices, contents, & availability subject to change without notice.
Disney charaters and artwork © Disney Enterprises, Inc.

09

SING WITH THE CHOIR

These GREAT COLLECTIONS let singers
BECOME PART OF A FULL CHOIR and sing along
with some of the most-loved songs of all time.
Each book includes SATB parts (arrangements are enlarged from octavo-size to 9" x 12")
and the accompanying CD features full, professionally recorded performances.

Now you just need to turn on the CD, open the book, pick your part, and
SING ALONG WITH THE CHOIR!

1. ANDREW LLOYD WEBBER
Any Dream Will Do • As If We Never Said Good-bye • Don't Cry for Me Argentina • Love Changes Everything • Memory • The Music of the Night • Pie Jesu • Whistle down the Wind.
00333001 Book/CD Pack $14.95

2. BROADWAY
Bring Him Home • Cabaret • For Good • Luck Be a Lady • Seasons of Love • There's No Business Like Show Business • Where Is Love? • You'll Never Walk Alone.
00333002 Book/CD Pack $14.95

3. STANDARDS
Cheek to Cheek • Georgia on My Mind • I Left My Heart in San Francisco • I'm Beginning to See the Light • Moon River • On the Sunny Side of the Street • Skylark • When I Fall in Love.
00333003 Book/CD Pack $14.95

4. THE 1950S
At the Hop • The Great Pretender • Kansas City • La Bamba • Love Me Tender • My Prayer • Rock Around the Clock • Unchained Melody.
00333004 Book/CD Pack $14.95

5. THE 1960S
All You Need is Love • Can't Help Falling in Love • Dancing in the Street • Good Vibrations • I Heard It Through the Grapevine • I'm a Believer • Under the Boardwalk • What a Wonderful World.
00333005 Book/CD Pack $14.95

6. THE 1970S
Ain't No Mountain High Enough • Bohemian Rhapsody • I'll Be There • Imagine • Let It Be • Night Fever • Yesterday Once More • You Are the Sunshine of My Life.
00333006 Book/CD Pack $14.95

7. DISNEY FAVORITES
The Bare Necessities • Be Our Guest • Circle of Life • Cruella De Vil • Friend like Me • Hakuna Matata • Joyful, Joyful • Under the Sea.
00333007 Book/CD Pack $14.95

8. DISNEY HITS
Beauty and the Beast • Breaking Free • Can You Feel the Love Tonight • Candle on the Water • Colors of the Wind • A Whole New World (Aladdin's Theme) • You'll Be in My Heart • You've Got a Friend in Me.
00333008 Book/CD Pack $14.95

9. LES MISÉRABLES
At the End of the Day • Bring Him Home • Castle on a Cloud • Do You Hear the People Sing? • Finale • I Dreamed a Dream • On My Own • One Day More.
00333009 Book/CD Pack $14.95

10. CHRISTMAS FAVORITES
Frosty the Snow Man • The Holiday Season • (There's No Place Like) Home for the Holidays • Little Saint Nick • Merry Christmas, Darling • Santa Claus Is Comin' to Town • Silver Bells • White Christmas.
00333011 Book/CD Pack $14.95

11. CHRISTMAS TIME IS HERE
Blue Christmas • Christmas Time is Here • Feliz Navidad • Happy Xmas (War Is Over) • I'll Be Home for Christmas • Let It Snow! Let It Snow! Let It Snow! • We Need a Little Christmas • Wonderful Christmastime.
00333012 Book/CD Pack $14.95

FOR MORE INFORMATION, SEE YOUR LOCAL MUSIC DEALER, OR WRITE TO:

HAL•LEONARD® CORPORATION
7777 W. BLUEMOUND RD. P.O. BOX 13819 MILWAUKEE, WI 53213

Prices, contents, and availability subject to change without notice.

0508